# HABIT STACKING

## 127 Small Changes to Improve Your Health, Wealth, and Happiness

### (The 2nd Edition)

Steve "S.J." Scott

www.DevelopGoodHabits.com

# Disclaimer

No part of this publication may be reproduced or transmitted in any form or by any means, mechanical or electronic, including photocopying or recording, or by any information storage and retrieval system, or transmitted by email without permission in writing from the publisher.

While all attempts have been made to verify the information provided in this publication, neither the author nor the publisher assumes any responsibility for errors, omissions, or contrary interpretations of the subject matter herein.

This book is for entertainment purposes only. The views expressed are those of the author alone, and should not be taken as expert instruction or commands. The reader is responsible for his or her own actions.

Adherence to all applicable laws and regulations, including international, federal, state, and local governing professional licensing, business practices, advertising, and all other aspects of doing business in the US, Canada, or any other jurisdiction is the sole responsibility of the purchaser or reader.

Neither the author nor the publisher assumes any responsibility or liability whatsoever on the behalf of the purchaser or reader of these materials.

Any perceived slight of any individual or organization is purely unintentional.

# Contents

# Your Free Gift

As a way of saying thanks for your purchase, I'm offering a free report that's exclusive to readers of *Habit Stacking*.

With the *Habit Stacking Quick Start Guide*, you'll discover a printable reference guide of all the rules, steps and a list of the 127 habits you can use to implement the following strategy. Everything you need to get started with habit stacking is included in **the PDF that's part of the free companion website**.

Go Here to Grab the Habit Stacking Quick Start Guide:
www.developgoodhabits.com/stacking_website

# Hyperlinks Included in This Book

The digital version of *Habit Stacking* includes over a hundred hyperlinks to resources and tools that can help you self-educate. But if I included them here, it would have resulted in a clunky reading experience (and also a frustrating one because some websites will change or delete their links in the future).

That's why I've compiled all the websites mentioned in *Habit Stacking* on my blog: www.developgoodhabits.com/habitstackingnotes

If you'd like to learn more about a specific tool or resource, then I recommend checking out this page and bookmarking it for future reference.

# Join the DGH Community

Looking to build your goal-specific habits? If so, then check out the Develop Good Habits (DGH) community: www.HabitsGroup.com

This is an excellent group full of like-minded individuals who focus on getting results with their lives. Here you can discover simple strategies for building powerful habits, find accountability partners, and ask questions about your struggles. If you want to "level up" the results from this book, then this is the place to be.

Just go to www.HabitsGroup.com to join the DGH Community.

# PART I

INTRODUCTION

# The Power of Small Actions

Imagine what life would be like if you began each day with **small actions that created a chain reaction of positive benefits throughout your life**.

You eat a healthy breakfast, have a great conversation with your loved ones, and then begin your workday focusing on the important tasks. Then, throughout the day, you complete other habits that positively impact your top goals. I guarantee you'd feel more fulfilled, get more accomplished, and have a better direction for your career.

All of this can be possible when you focus on small actions that relate to *your* important goals.

These habits don't require much effort. In fact, most only take **five minutes or less to complete**. But they have a powerful compounding effect if you repeat them often enough. This can include making a healthy drink, writing a loving message to a loved one, or identifying three important tasks to work on first thing in the morning. Do any of these repeatedly and you'll notice a vast improvement in your health, relationships, and work productivity.

Think of what your life would be like if your entire day was filled with these small actions. Wouldn't your life improve *without* a whole lot of effort? I bet it would!

## A Five-Minute Exercise to Transform Your Relationships

It's easy to disregard the power of small actions. You might think that a simple task *can't* make a difference in your life. If you feel this way, then I challenge you to complete a simple exercise that, coincidentally, only requires five minutes of your time.

Right now, there is someone in your life who you love with all your heart. This could be a spouse, romantic partner, parent, child, or close friend. He or she means the world to you, but maybe you haven't said that lately. Right now (or sometime today), I want you to **tell this person that you love them**.

The method for doing this is up to you. It could be on the phone, in person, or through a short note. Heck, you could even send a text message if you're shy about how this message will be received. Simply tell this person, in a few sentences, how much he or she means to you.

I'm serious here.

**Stop reading this book right now and talk to that special someone in your life!**

I'll wait for you …

…

…

…

…

…

Okay, you're back!

So, what was it like to express your feelings to someone you love? I imagine it felt pretty awesome!

How long did it take to complete this simple exercise? A few minutes or so? Or was it maybe longer because the conversation started flowing?

Now, think about what life would be like if this were a daily habit. You could repeat this action for every important person in your life, sending them thoughtful messages full of warmth and love.

The method you choose for expressing these feelings is irrelevant. It could be a phone call, handwritten message, Post-it note, text message, or eCard if this person lives far away. The only important thing is to do it!

Consider how this would positively impact your relationships. The people you care for would start their days hearing loving messages. *You* would start your day knowing that you've brightened the day of someone important.

All of this is possible when you add small actions to your day.

## Small Actions Create Success

We've all heard that story of the overnight success. This is the story of the musician who records a double-platinum debut album, or the startup CEO who sells his company for a billion dollars, or the average Joe who hits the multimillion-dollar lottery jackpot. Our society loves stories about ordinary people who achieve amazing results with seemingly very little effort.

Unfortunately, the story of the overnight success is nothing more than a myth. For every person who strikes it rich, there are *thousands* of folks who languish in obscurity.

The cause of all this is **the belief that *success is an event*.** That you can transition from "zero to hero" without a lot of effort. That you can start as a nobody, get discovered by the right person who notices your unique talent, and suddenly skyrocket up the ranks of the rich and famous.

Unfortunately, this story of the overnight success rarely happens in real life.

If you took the time to talk to any successful person, she would tell you that **success is always a process.** It's a daily slog where most of your time is spent doing the same thing over and over. Rinse and repeat. Day in and day out. A few wins along the way, and then a few setbacks. Eventually, by working hard, and often for many, *many* years, you'll become successful.

That's the reality of success. It's not luck or an event—just a lot of hard work and daily action.

Or, to borrow a famous quote that's commonly attributed to Thomas Jefferson:

**"I'm a great believer in luck. The harder I work, the more luck I have."**

The people who succeed in the game of life understand the important power of small actions. They flourish by doing two critical things well:

» Identifying the most important activities (or habits) related to their goals.

» Repeating these activities **every day**.

Simply put, when you know the important tasks related to your goal and do them continuously, you'll surpass the folks who spend their time making excuses about why they're not successful.

To quote Jeff Olson, from his book *The Slight Edge*:

"The truth is, what you do matters. What you do *today* matters. What you do *every day* matters. Successful people ... do things that seem to make no difference at all in the act of doing them, and they do them over and over and over until the compound effect kicks in."

That compound effect that Olson talks about can be achieved by introducing small actions into your life.

## The Importance of Small Actions

The little things will have a positive *or* negative impact on every area of your life. Just think back to the example from before. I talked about how the consistency of sending a nice message to your loved ones will vastly improve your interpersonal relationships.

Now, imagine what would happen if you sent a message of love *just* to your spouse.

Every. Single. Day.

I guarantee the quality of your relationship would skyrocket.

In contrast, imagine the opposite of this scenario. Each day you ignore, mock, and belittle your spouse. Do this once or twice and it'll be somewhat damaging to your relationship. But I *guarantee* that if this were your daily routine, you would eventually win a one-way ticket to divorce city.

One article that I recently read supports this idea. The author talked about why it's important to "sweat the small stuff." In fact, you should look for those small bids for emotional connection by giving attention, interest, affection, and support to the important people in your life. Really, all the people in your life need are the small gestures that show you care.

Now, the interesting thing about small actions is how surprisingly easy they are to complete. Usually they only take a few minutes to do, yet they are often pushed aside because they don't seem immediately important—like that nine o'clock presentation for your job.

Even worse: a small action is often overlooked due to its level of ease.

You can convince yourself that you'll "get around" to it. The task doesn't require much effort, so you never feel the need to schedule it into your day. Unfortunately, what usually happens is you end the day without doing it. This is what I call the "I'll remember to do it" paradox.

## The "I'll Remember To Do It" Paradox

How many times have you told yourself that you'll remember to complete a task, only to realize *hours later* that you never got around to it?

It might be a quick errand, a simple task, or even a habit that only requires a few minutes of your time (like taking a vitamin or flossing your teeth).

Some actions seem so easy to complete that you don't feel it's important to create a reminder to do them. *They're too small to fail.* But let me ask you this: how many times have you followed through on one of these simple tasks? I bet not very often.

That's the paradox when it comes to these small habits. They're super easy to do, but they get overlooked because there isn't an immediate negative consequence for not completing them.

While each small action doesn't require much effort, you still need a framework that will guarantee that you do it 100% of the time.

Specifically, **each action requires a reminder to complete it.** That said, if you filled your life with dozens of alerts, alarms, and Post-it notes, then you'd probably drive yourself crazy with a feeling of overwhelm. That's why I recommend grouping these small actions together, using a concept I call *habit stacking*.

# Habit Stacking: A Quick Definition

As you've probably experienced, it's *not easy* to build new habits. You already have many tasks in your life, with an ever-increasing list of obligations. So it might seem impossible to add something new to your daily routine. It's my contention that not only do you have enough time to build a single new habit, but it's possible to add dozens of habits to your busy day without it negatively impacting your life. All you need to do is:

1.  Identify those small important actions (like writing a loving message to the important people in your life).
2.  Group them together into a routine with equally important actions.
3.  Schedule a specific time each day to complete this routine.
4.  Use a trigger as a reminder to complete this stack.
5.  Make it super easy to get started.

**In essence, the goal here is to complete the habits that you know are important by stacking them on top of one another.**

Habit. Stacking.

Sounds simple, right?

Habit stacking works because you eliminate the stress of adding too many new things to your life. Instead, you begin with a few simple but effective habits and then build on them as this routine becomes an important "can't miss" part of your day.

This stack (and the others you build) will become as important as the routines you follow when you get up in the morning, prepare for work, and get ready to sleep.

This is what I hope to teach you in this book, *Habit Stacking: 127 Small Changes to Improve Your Health, Wealth, and Happiness.*

## About Habit Stacking

The purpose of this book is to help you identify the important small actions in your life and build them into your daily routine—*without* causing you to feel overwhelmed by this change.

That's why I break down the content into **twelve distinct sections**:

**Part I** is the current section you're reading, which provides an overview of habit stacking and why small actions matter.

**Part II** talks about goals. Specifically, why they are important, how to create ones that match what you want from life, and how they relate to the three types of habits we'll cover in this book.

**Part III** briefly covers the psychology behind habit stacking and how you can use it to remember all those small life-changing actions.

**Part IV** shows you how to get started with habit stacking. Here, I provide nine rules for creating a stack and the thirteen-step process for building your first routine.

**Part V** is the beginning of the seven sections that cover the 127 habits. We'll start with career goals, which will focus on improving your productivity, increasing your business revenue, and implementing the habits that help you do better at your job.

**Part VI** will cover the finance habits, which will include topics like saving for retirement, improving your credit score, eliminating your credit card debt, and investing to build long-term wealth.

**Part VII** goes over the health habits that are important for maintaining a balance of physical fitness, eating the right foods, and practicing specific routines that ensure the safety of you and your family.

**Part IIX** discusses the leisure habits that might not seem immediately important but are vital for improving the quality of your life.

**Part IX** talks about the organizing habits that provide structure to your surroundings in a mindful way where you don't feel overwhelmed by the "stuff" in your life.

**Part X** will cover the relationship goals that help you enhance interactions with the important individuals in your life, while encouraging you to meet new people.

**Part XI** includes spiritual habits, which covers a wide range of topics like meditation, prayer, yoga, helping others, or reciting affirmations.

**Part XII** provides nine examples of habit stacks you can build and how to overcome the six challenges you might encounter when building a routine, and then we'll wrap up the book.

While you might feel tempted to skip ahead to the "good stuff" that starts in Part V, I recommend reading this book in sequential order. Each section builds on what you've learned in the previous one. That means that by the time you get to the description of the individual habits, you'll be able to accurately choose the actions that have the biggest benefit for your life.

## About the Author

Before getting started, let me introduce myself and tell you a brief story about the origin of the habit stacking concept.

My name is Steve "S.J." Scott. I run the blog Develop Good Habits, and I'm the author of a series of habit-related titles, all of which are available at HabitBooks.com.

The purpose of my content is to show how *continuous* habit development can lead to a better life. Instead of lecturing you, I provide simple strategies that are easy to use no matter how busy you get during the day.

My discovery of the habit stacking concept was a complete accident. It was inspired by a moment of utter frustration about a not-so-great situation and what I did to fix it. Let me explain.

In 2012, I had been dating a wonderful woman (who is now my wife) for a year. We had a good relationship but also a challenging one because we lived almost two hours apart. Due to her job as a schoolteacher and my need to have a dedicated space for my business, our time together was limited. This meant we only saw each other on weekends and holidays.

Now, if you've ever been in a long-distance relationship, you know that a lengthy time apart can be a major source of tension. You want to be with this person, but it's not easy to make that happen. Often, this tension leads to disagreements, misunderstandings, and eventually arguments.

Finally, we reached the point where we had to progress as a couple *or* break up.

## It's Not Me, It's *You*

One day, we sat down and had an honest talk. I loved her and truly didn't want the relationship to end. But we also realized that our interactions were far from perfect.

During this conversation, my future wife told me something that I think was very profound. She said, "Steve, it's not the time apart that's the issue. It's the feeling that you don't even think about me when I'm not around."

Ouch.

Trust me, it was *extremely* hard to hear that bit of feedback.

But it was also a light-bulb moment. It made me realize how little effort I was putting into nurturing our relationship during the workweek. Sure, there was an occasional phone call, but there were many days when we didn't talk to each other.

She went on to say something else that was equally profound: "Sometimes, all I need from you is a simple text message or phone call. It doesn't have to be long, just something that lets me know you love me and that you're thinking of me."

This statement made me realize that sometimes it's the smallest of actions that can have the biggest impact on someone's life. After *truly* hearing what my girlfriend was saying, I made the internal commitment to send her a nice text and phone call every day without fail.

See the simplicity here?

To improve my relationship, all I had to do was build two habits that took a whopping total of fifteen minutes each day:

1. Send one loving text message first thing in the morning.
2. Make time for a ten-minute phone call in the evening.

It's such an easy solution that can be broken down into a simple mathematical formula (if you're a geek like me):

## 1 loving text message + 1 daily phone call = happy girlfriend

Of course, all this sounds easy in theory. As strange as it sounds, I quickly realized that the most difficult thing to remember was sending that text message first thing in the morning. It took less than a minute to do, but it kept slipping my mind because I'd wake up each day with a to-do list full of "important" tasks.

Eventually, I found a solution: I set a reminder on my phone that dinged during the first thirty minutes of my day. When the alarm went off, I would send a nice message. Real romantic, right?

Fast forward a few weeks to the day when I had a random thought: Since I was *already* consistently completing a small, positive habit each morning, why couldn't I add a few more to this routine?

So, I decided to schedule a thirty-minute block of time into my day when I would complete a bunch of quick but important habits. These included making a nutritious shake, reviewing my goals, researching the market for my business, and jotting down the three priority tasks for the day. Each task took less than five minutes to do, yet they improved my life because they directly aligned with my important goals.

In 2014, I started talking about this concept on my blog (calling it habit stacking) and even published a book that showed others how they can incorporate this routine into their days.

## Habit Stacking: 2017 and Beyond

Currently, my life is *very different* from when I first started habit stacking. My girlfriend is now my wife. I now live in the town that was once two hours away from my old apartment. And we have an incredible eleven-month-old son, who I take care of in the morning hours when it's just the two of us. We like to call it "Daddy Daycare."

What *hasn't* changed is my adherence to habit stacking. Sure, I've swapped out many actions, but I still start my day by completing a daily routine full of small tasks that directly relate to important goals.

I'll share more about this routine in Part IV, but for now, let's talk about what's different in this second edition, and then we'll dive into the meat of the book.

## About Habit Stacking: The Second Edition

The book you're reading is the second edition of *Habit Stacking*. I wrote the original back in April 2014, simply describing a routine that I personally enjoyed every day.

While many readers *loved* the concept, others absolutely hated it. They had two major complaints:

1.  The habit stacking concept wasn't explained fully enough.
2.  Some small actions seemed overly simplistic.

While I feel this routine has been valuable to me, I had to admit to myself that I didn't do a thorough enough job describing *how* it can help others.

All of this led to my decision to publish a revised version of the original book.

My first inclination was to add a few minor updates. But as I got feedback from readers, I realized the book required a complete overhaul, with more explanations and better examples. As a result, this second edition:

» Is twice as long, with a clear explanation of how habit stacking can benefit you

» Details 127 small actions with specific resources to get started

» Shows how to build habits that stick

» Provides examples of specific stacks you can build

» Includes a free companion website full of bonus material that will assist with your habit stacking efforts

Even if you've already read the first edition, I guarantee you'll learn many new things in this updated second edition. Not only will you rediscover the benefits of habit stacking, you will also learn the most effective way to immediately implement this routine into your busy life.

## About the Apps and Resources

You'll quickly notice that this book is chock-full of links to many resources, apps, and websites. They're included here because they can help you implement the concepts mentioned in this book.

If you're someone who likes to leverage technology to build habits, then I recommend checking them out. That said, if you're not really into apps, then feel free to ignore these suggestions. You'll find that this book follows a "choose your own adventure" model where you use what you like and disregard the rest.

Finally, you don't have to write down resources mentioned in this book because all of them are also included on the companion website.

## Getting Started with Habit Stacking

Habit stacking has transformed my life. I no longer worry about *when* I'll complete a small but important action. Instead, I identify the best time and then I add it to one of my existing stacks. This allows me to stay on top of my important goals without loading up my day full of annoying reminders.

If you're ready to build small actions that will transform your life, then read on to discover the power of habit stacking. To kick things off, we're going to talk about the importance of setting goals and how to identify the right habits for you.

# PART II

## GOALS AND HOW THEY RELATE TO HABITS

# Why Goals Are Important

The best way to build a habit stack is to combine actions related to what you want from life. In other words, it makes no sense to add random habits together that have no personal meaning. Instead, each must align with your goals. This will make it easier to stick with a new habit stacking routine.

We all have different goals, so there is no right answer for what habits are important. But it's been my experience that almost every task can fit neatly into one of these seven categories:

1. **Career goals** focus on improving your productivity, increasing your business revenue, or climbing up the proverbial corporate ladder. Whether you're looking to improve a specific work-related skill or streamline your business, career goals are important because they have a direct impact on the other six areas of your life.

2. **Finance goals** will increase in importance as you get older. These actions include saving for retirement, improving your credit score, eliminating your credit card debt, and investing to build long-term wealth.

3. **Health goals** help you maintain a balance of physical fitness and eating the right foods. There are many subcategories that are included here, like losing weight, improving your diet, eating different types of foods, or becoming more physically active.

4. **Leisure goals** relate to personally significant activities. Often, we feel overwhelmed by everything else in life, so we procrastinate on those "bucket list" items that don't seem

immediately important. However, the best way to improve the quality of your life is to set goals that relate to the fun stuff. These activities can include planning vacations, spending time with your family, or focusing on a hobby like home brewing, hunting, cooking, or painting.

5. **Organizing goals** help you structure your surroundings in a mindful way so you don't feel overwhelmed by the "stuff" in your life. This includes basic ideas for regularly cleaning your immediate environment, and it also goes into how to remove the items that no longer give you any personal satisfaction.

6. **Relationships goals** are about enhancing relationships with your significant other, family members, or friends. You could also set goals to improve your social skills, find a romantic partner, or simply become a better person to everyone you meet.

7. **Spirituality goals** have a different meaning for each of us. They could include activities like meditation, prayer, yoga, helping others, or reciting affirmations. Basically, whatever helps you achieve a calm peace of mind can be categorized as a spiritual goal.

As you can see, there are many goals you can set. That's why you should understand what's truly important to you. You can do this by asking yourself a series of questions, which we'll cover next.

# 12 Goal-Specific Questions to Ask Yourself

When creating goals, it's important to identify what you want from life. You only have a little time each day to make things happen, so you should focus on the tasks that give you the biggest bang for your buck.

That's why I recommend a simple exercise to identify those important habits. If you answer the following twelve questions, then you can successfully identify the small actions that will go into your daily stacks:

1. *"Is there a small habit that can support a major habit?"* (For example, packing your exercise clothes in the morning so they'll be ready for the gym in the evening.)

2. *"Do I often end the day frustrated because I didn't complete the most important tasks?"* (Identify the most important tasks for the next day and then schedule them into your calendar.)

3. *"What quick activities make me feel inspired or happy?"* (For example, watching a short motivational video each morning.)

4. *"What five goals are the most important to me right now?"* (What can you do daily to support all five of these goals?)

5. *"What are the activities that I love to do?"* (Think of tasks that can support hobbies, like running, knitting, traveling, or reading.)

6. *"What areas of my financial life do I need to improve?"* (If you're in debt, then address this first. But if you have money in the

bank, then you should build a habit that focuses on building up your investment portfolio.)

7. *"Can I improve the quality of my interpersonal relationships?"* (Think about your interactions with your parents, children, significant other, and closest friends. Is there anything you can do daily to make these interactions better?)

8. *"What makes me feel great about myself?"* (If something brings you enjoyment, then you should either do it every day or schedule time for it each week.)

9. *"How can I become more spiritual in my daily life?"* (For example, read from a book of prayers, practice a bit of yoga, or recite positive affirmations.)

10. *"What is a new skill I've always wanted to master?"* (For example, make a habit of researching and learning about talents like home brewing, playing a musical instrument, learning a new language, or anything that sounds fun.)

11. *"Is there anything I can do to support my local community or an important cause?"* (We all believe in something. So if you schedule time daily for this activity, then it's not hard to consistently help others.)

12. "Is there something that I can do to improve my job performance and get a raise?" (For example, build a skill that will become valuable to the company.)

These are just a few questions to ask yourself that will help you identify goal-specific habits. Really, it's a simple process of knowing what truly matters to you and building a routine that supports your life.

This means knowing what *you* want. A better relationship? Increased productivity? More fun? Less stress?

Your answer will be vastly different from the thousands of other people who read this book. And that's why I believe everyone's habit stack is unique from person to person.

The tricky part is that not everyone automatically knows what habits are important, which is why I've included an exhaustive list of 127 small actions in Parts V through XI. But before we get to that, let's talk about the different types of habits and how they fit into a habit stack.

# 3 Types of Habits
# (and Why Each Is Important)

Not all habits are equal. You have simple ones, like brushing your teeth or kissing your spouse before heading off to work. You have complex ones that often require constant willpower, like avoiding certain foods or exercising every day. And in between, there are the small habits that have a positive (or negative) compounding effect on your life.

The mistake people make is they don't take the time to understand what it takes to build habits. Some are easy to master, like the three-minute habit of writing down your daily goals. Others are extremely difficult to make "sticky," like a thirty-minute exercise habit.

That's why it's important to create a distinction between the different habits that you're trying to form. Specifically, when it comes to habit stacking, I feel there are three types of habits that you should add to a routine:

1. Keystone habits
2. Support habits
3. Elephant habits

You'll soon discover that most of the habits included in this book are support habits, but you need to understand the difference between each so you can pick the right ones for your situation.

## 1. Keystone Habits

Keystone habits are a powerful concept that Charles Duhigg discussed in this book The Power of Habit: Why We Do What We Do in Life and Business. Simply put, a keystone habit can have a positive impact on **multiple areas** of your life—even if you're not intentionally trying to improve them.

A common example that people use is a **thirty-minute daily exercise routine**. Let's say you start running to lose a few pounds. As you get fitter, you subconsciously start to avoid fatty and sugary foods, so your weight dramatically decreases. This improves your self-esteem, which creates a positive change in both your relationships and your career (because you now feel confident enough to ask for a raise).

On the surface, *all* you did was exercise for thirty minutes every day, but the addition of this single habit caused a chain reaction of positive results. That's the essence of a keystone habit—it's a single change that produces a positive trickle-down effect in other areas of your life.

Now, the reason I used exercise to explain this concept is because it has always been one of my major keystone habits. In fact, it's also the example that Duhigg provides in his book.

To quote Duhigg, "Typically, people who exercise start eating better and becoming more productive at work. They smoke less and show more patience with colleagues and family. They use their credit cards less frequently and say they feel less stressed … exercise is a keystone habit that triggers widespread change."

There are many varieties of keystone habits. Some require a lengthy commitment of time (like thirty to sixty minutes daily), while others only take a few minutes to complete.

There are many examples of great keystone habits that can include meditating, tracking your expenditures, planning your day, and scheduling regular meals with your family. As you can see, some of these might only require a few minutes of your time, while others require longer than an hour.

So therein lies the problem. Since we all have a limited amount of time, it's impossible to continuously add thirty-minute blocks of new activities to your already busy day. Eventually, you have to choose the habits that are most important to you and make sure they get *completed* before anything else.

## EXAMPLE

For instance, I only focus on five keystone habits each day:

1. Completing a habit stacking routine
2. Writing for at least thirty minutes
3. Finishing three work-related tasks
4. Exercising for at least thirty minutes
5. Reading at least two pages of a nonfiction book

Allow me to briefly review each of the five to show why they're important.

**Habit stacking** enables me to consistently complete all the support and elephant habits that we'll talk about throughout this book. These are the small activities that are important but impossible to consistently remember without a reminder (like journaling, reviewing my goals, and drinking thirty-two ounces of water to start the day).

**Writing** is the cornerstone of my online business, so it impacts my income, personal fulfillment, and relaxation. The more writing I can do daily, the more "in control" I feel about my daily routine.

**Finishing three work-related tasks** is another keystone habit related to my business. After writing, I'll look at current projects in my Todoist app. The goal here is simple—I identify and complete the next tasks to move these projects forward.

Sometimes, a task only takes a few minutes to complete. Other times, it'll require a few hours. The important thing (for me) is to consistently make progress on these time-sensitive projects.

**Exercising** has a positive impact on *every* area of my life. When I consistently work out, I feel happier, more relaxed, and more productive. Sure, this activity requires a daily commitment, but it also helps me achieve goals in all seven of the categories that I mentioned in the previous section.

**Reading nonfiction** has a positive impact on both my business and creativity. I find that the more I read, the more I'm able to come up with interesting ideas to include in my writing. Basically, it's a case of quality in = quality out.

All five actions are my personal keystone habits because they benefit all the areas of my life. The total daily time I spend on them is three to four hours. Yes, that might seem like a lot of time for habits, but I feel that I accomplish more during this time than most people can do with their standard eight-hour workday.

If you'd like to build keystone habits into your life, then I recommend getting started with the ones identified as such in Parts V through XI, where we go over the individual habits. Or, if you want a quick shortcut, then I recommend checking out the list of keystone habits listed in the free companion course.

## 2. Support Habits

Not every habit can be a priority. In fact, you can only focus on a handful of keystone habits before you'll feel overwhelmed, which is why it's important to form "support habits."

These cleverly titled habits do exactly as they are described—**they support the achievement of an important keystone habit**.

I'll admit that the difference between these two concepts might be confusing, so let me give you a quick illustration of how they differ from one another.

I've already talked about how exercise is one of my keystone habits. The thing to remember here is it's *not* an isolated action. In fact, I've had to build many smaller "support habits" that help me make sure that I rarely miss an exercise day. Specifically, there are seven habits that support this routine:

1. Check the weather forecast to see if I need to exercise outdoors or at the gym.
2. Plan my schedule each morning, specifically asking two questions:
   » "What time will I run today?"
   » "What clothes do I need to bring with me?"

3.  Pack my exercise clothes in the morning before leaving the house (just in case I decide to go to a Starbucks coffeehouse in the afternoon).

4.  Drink sixty-four ounces of water to make sure I'm properly hydrated for my runs.

5.  Weigh myself each morning (during marathon-training season).

6.  Record each run in my Runner's Log app.

7.  Wear my Fitbit to count my daily steps.

As you can see, many small actions and decisions are made each day *just* to make sure I complete an exercise routine. Each only requires a minute or two of action, but they're just as important as any other habit because they eliminate those excuses that people make when they skip a workout (e.g., "I didn't pack the right clothes" or "I planned a run but didn't know there would be a lightning storm in the afternoon").

Now, if I relied on memory alone to complete each of these seven actions, then I'd probably miss something important *at least* one day a week. But since all seven are part of my "exercise habit stack," I can be confident that nothing will slip through the cracks.

Never underestimate the power of support habits. While they only take a few minutes to do, they are the glue that holds together your keystone habits.

## 3. Elephant Habits

We've all heard this piece of advice before:

"How do you eat an elephant? One bite at a time."

The idea here is that whenever you're faced with a large, complex goal, all you need to do is chip away at it in small chunks.

Unfortunately, many people don't apply this mindset to their lives. When they're forced to tackle large projects, they procrastinate or even avoid them completely because the tasks seem insurmountable.

You, on the other hand, can take any large project and chip away it using what I call **elephant habits**.

Elephant habits are designed to overcome the natural resistance that we all feel whenever we're forced to do a potentially unpleasant task. You know it must be done, but you avoid starting because dedicating a few days to it sounds as fun as getting a root canal.

Like the quote mentioned before, an elephant habit will help you complete a project one bite at a time.

The goal here is to chip away at a simple but time-consuming project in five- to fifteen-minute daily increments. You can do this with many of the larger tasks on your to-do list:

- » Decluttering your home
- » Packing for a move
- » Organizing your paperwork (like before tax season)
- » Studying for an exam
- » Completing a time-consuming homework assignment
- » Reading a difficult book

I use elephant habits all the time whenever I'm faced with something unpleasant. Rather than building it up in my mind as a horrific ordeal, I overcome inertia by scheduling a five- to ten-minute daily block where I can chip away at the project. (Usually, it's tacked on to an existing habit stack.)

Elephant habits have a similar framework to the **mini-habits concept** that we'll discuss later. When you tell yourself that a task "only" takes five minutes of your time, it's easier to convince yourself to get started. And what usually happens is, once you get started, you'll find yourself doing more of that activity than you originally planned.

Well, that's a brief overview of the three types of habits I'll discuss in this book, so let's start talking about what happens when you group together these small but important actions.

Specifically, I'll talk about two problems people have with building small habits and how habit stacking is the perfect solution for overcoming them.

# PART III

## THE PSYCHOLOGY OF HABIT STACKING

# Problem #1: "I often don't feel motivated."

Let's start this section on the psychology of habit stacking by talking about the **two main problems that people have with building habits** and how this strategy can become the perfect solution for overcoming them.

We've all done this. You decide to change your life, so you set a major goal and try to build a specific habit (or habits) to help you achieve this outcome. You're perfect for a few days until life gets in the way, which leads to skipping a day. The pattern repeats itself. Good for a few days, then miss one or two. Eventually, you quit in frustration because you simply can't make this new habit stick.

Let me be honest here—it's *not* easy to build habits. Sure, many experts will tell you that it's a simple matter of identifying a change and then doing it daily. However, it's one thing to *read* about forming habits, but it's a whole other thing to create a permanent change.

We all live hectic lives, so it's hard to do anything consistently, and it's even more challenging trying to fit something new into your already hectic schedule.

In fact, you might be asking yourself:

"How can I build a new routine when I've already failed in the past?"

Well, the answer comes down to *motivation*. Specifically, how much reliance you place on motivation alone in order to get things done.

## The Myth of Motivation

I'm going to come right out and say it: ***motivation alone does not work.***

Sure, you can listen to upbeat music or read an inspiring quote to create an energized state. But it's a temporary feeling. Motivation won't get you through those times when you're tired and uninterested in working at an important goal.

Let me explain.

In the book Willpower, authors Roy F. Baumeister and John Tierney described a concept known as **ego depletion,** which is a person's "diminished capacity to regulate their thoughts, feelings, and actions."

Simply put, our willpower is like a muscle. It weakens throughout the day because of constant use.

Baumeister and his colleagues have tested ego depletion in a variety of scenarios. One was called the radish experiment. Here, they brought three groups of people into a room and offered a selection of food (before working on a puzzle): pieces of chocolate, warm cookies, and radishes.

> » One group could eat anything they wanted.
> » Another group could only eat the radishes.
> » The final group wasn't given any food options.

After that, each group was moved into a separate room, where they had to work on a challenging puzzle. The groups that didn't previously exert willpower (i.e., they ate whatever they wanted or weren't given a food option) worked on the puzzle for an *average of twenty minutes.* The group that had to exert willpower and resist the tasty treats worked on the puzzle for an *average of eight minutes.*

What does the experiment show?

It's simple: most people can resist temptations, but this effort leaves us in a "weakened" condition where it becomes harder to tap into that pool of willpower. People don't achieve peak results with a task because of motivation. Instead, the number of decisions and completed tasks ultimately determine their level of success with a new task.

This leads to two important lessons that will ultimately determine your success at forming habits:

» You have a finite amount of willpower that becomes depleted as you use it.

» You use the same stock of willpower for all manner of tasks.

It's important to recognize that your levels of willpower (and therefore motivation) will decrease as the day goes on. This means that if you'd like to make any significant, lasting change in your life, you need to schedule it as early in your day as possible.

In fact, Kelly McGonigal, author of *The Willpower Instinct*, found that the best time to work on a high-priority activity is first thing in the morning because that's when we're at our freshest. And then your ability to work on complex tasks diminishes as the day wears on.

This leads to another problem that people have when trying to build habits, which we'll cover next.

# Problem #2: "I can't remember to complete many small actions."

I've talked at length about why small actions are important. So the question is, *why* do people struggle to complete them on a consistent basis?

I don't think it's because we're lazy or unmotivated or can't find the time. Instead, the difficulty is related to a concept called *cognitive load*.

Let me explain.

We all have a finite limit on our short-term memory. It's been said that most people can only retain **seven chunks of information**. Since a tiny fraction of what you know is stored in your "working memory," you have to rely on long-term memory and existing habits to accomplish almost every task in life.

For instance, when you first learned how to drive a car, you had to consciously think about the process required for each action and decision. This included tasks like changing lanes, parallel parking, using a turn signal, or driving with a stick shift. Each task required constant reinforcement of your short-term memory.

Eventually, these actions became learned behavior, which means you no longer have to think about the process required to drive a car. You just do it! This frees up your mind so you can focus other things, like singing an off-key version of your favorite song on Spotify.

**Now, let's use a different example to demonstrate cognitive load.** We all know that tracking your expenses is the key to mastering your financial life. Honestly, it's not hard to write down an expenditure—it's an action that takes a few seconds to complete. But it's easy to forget because it's not an automatic part of your daily routine. If you don't use what's called a "trigger" to remind you of this action, then tracking your spending is hard to remember on a consistent basis.

Let's compare tracking expenditures to a small habit that's (hopefully) a permanent behavior—brushing your teeth.

We all know there are serious negative consequences if you forget this activity. Gingivitis, periodontitis, and tooth decay all are possibilities when you fail to stick to the daily teeth-brushing habit.

Your average person understands these risks, so she remembers to do it (at least) twice a day—usually in the morning and evening.

So, my question is, how do you remember to brush those pearly whites?

Well, I think the main reason is because this small action is usually "anchored" to a larger routine that you complete when you wake up in the morning and before you go to bed in the evening. Brushing your teeth doesn't strain your cognitive load because it's now an automatic action.

This leads to my next question: Why is it easy to remember brushing your teeth but harder to remember an equally important habit, like tracking your expenditures?

I feel the answer is related to the fact that tracking your expenditures isn't anchored to an existing routine, which is the main reason why it's important to build habit stacking routines into your day. So, let's talk about that next.

# Solution: Use Habit Stacking to Build Powerful Routines

Here's the essence of a habit stacking routine: You identify the small actions that relate to a goal or an important desired outcome. Next, you put these habits into a step-by-step routine that's completed in a logical sequence. Finally, you use proven psychological strategies to make this routine "sticky" so you never miss a day.

Habit stacking works for many reasons, but here are three main benefits:

1. You don't have to remember each small action because it's written down and part of an established routine. This frees up your mind to worry about other parts of your day.

2. You can easily do these habits because they're simple actions that don't take a lot of brainpower to complete. All you need is a sequential checklist where each action becomes a prompt for the next one.

3. You can add or subtract actions based on what you need to do that day. So if you wake up one morning with a miles-long to-do list, then you can skip the habits that aren't that important. Really, the only important thing is to do at least one of the habits in your stack. Consistency is key here!

Habit stacking can transform your life because you no longer worry about when you'll complete those small but important actions. You simply add them to a routine and make that commitment to do them every day.

Furthermore, repeating the same positive actions daily can have an amazing impact on your long-term goals. In the book *The Compound Effect*, author Darren Hardy explains it best with a simple formula:

"Small, Smart Choices + Consistency + Time = RADICAL DIFFERENCE"

To demonstrate this concept, let me give you five examples of how simple actions can help you in any area of your life.

## 5 Examples of Small Actions

***Want to write a book?*** Let's say you *only* have a spare twenty minutes to write each day, producing an average of three hundred words. Most people would give up before even getting started because they'd make the "I don't have enough time to write" excuse.

However, if you committed to *just* twenty minutes every day, you could produce 9,000 words a month, or a total of 108,000 words in a year. That's enough time to write *and* fully edit a standard-size novel. Not bad at all for just a few minutes of your spare time.

***Want to lose weight?*** You can maintain a food log and write down everything you eat. The core benefit here is *accountability*. When you know that you must record every item put into your mouth, you'll skip the occasional sweet or piece of junk food. Repeat this process enough times and you'll steadily lose weight—*without* going on a diet.

***Want to improve your career success?*** One small habit is to start each day by identifying two or three priority tasks and then write them down on a Post-it note. These should be activities that have the biggest impact on your career. If you can begin the day with a focus on these items, you'll do more "deep work" than the coworker who spends the first half hour answering emails or checking Facebook.

***Want to improve your sales numbers?*** Start by organizing your prospect list in order of priority. Then begin your day by contacting the "hot leads" that need the most attention, and then work your way down the list to the dead leads or people who simply won't respond to your phone calls.

***Want to get more dates?*** You can do this by expanding your social network. One small habit that can help is to start a conversation with a new person every day. It could be a coworker, a person in class or even a perfect stranger. Sure, you might be rebuffed or rejected, but this will give you an increased level of confidence that talking to new people isn't difficult.

These are just a handful of goal-specific actions that only require a small daily time investment. Imagine what your life would be like if you repeated this strategy for every area of your life. I guarantee you'd experience a major breakthrough.

So far, we've talked about habit stacking in vague terms. To help you understand what goes into one of these routines, let me provide an example from my current routine, and then we'll dive into the rules for building your first stack.

# PART IV

GETTING STARTED WITH
HABIT STACKING

# My Habit Stacking Routine
# (11 Small Actions)

As we've discussed, a habit stack is unique to the individual. In fact, I don't think it's a good idea to copy exactly what someone else does because we all have different goals. That said, I feel it's important for you to see an example of how this strategy works, while explaining the mindset behind each small action. In this section, **we'll go over my habit stacking routine.**

If you read the first edition, then you might notice that some of my habits are completely different now. That's because I'm now married and have an eleven-month-old son, whom I have to take care of each morning. So my goals, tasks, and overall schedule have definitely changed in the three years since publishing the previous edition.

With that out of the way, let's go over the eleven small habits that I complete for my morning stack. For each example, I've included a brief description of why it's personally important, how long it takes to complete, and what "goal category" it fulfills.

## Habit 1: Weigh Myself

Time required: One minute

Goal fulfilled: Health

The first thing I do in the morning is go into the bathroom and weigh myself. This is a support habit because it's related to my long-*long*-term goal of completing fifty marathons in fifty states (eighteen down, thirty-two to go!). Each year I try to complete two or three of these races. This means I need to carefully monitor my weight to make sure I'm near my target weight for each race: 165 to 170 pounds (or 75 to 77 kilograms).

This daily weigh-in acts as accountability for my snacking tendencies. Knowing I must step onto a scale each morning is often the one thing that'll prevent me from enjoying too many chips, cookies, or the "pint of no return."

## Habit 2: Fill up a 32-Ounce Bottle with Lemon Water

Time required: One minute

Goal fulfilled: Health

After the weigh-in, I'll walk downstairs into my kitchen and pour thirty-two ounces of ice-cold water with lemon into a Contigo water bottle. Why lemon? Because it promotes hydration, is a good source of vitamin C, and supports weight loss. Why the thirty-two-ounce bottle of water? Because it helps me stay on top of my daily water intake. I know drinking two of them throughout the day will give me the basic amount of water that people typically require.

## Habit 3: Start a Kettle of Tea

Time required: One minute

Goal fulfilled: Relationships

My wife loves a nice cup of tea in the morning. So, I'll start a kettle, which is usually ready by the time I complete the next habit. That way, by the time my wife comes downstairs, she has a steaming cup ready for her.

Remember: Sometimes it's the small things that count when it comes to strengthening a relationship.

## Habit 4: Do the Dishes

Time required: Five minutes

Goal fulfilled: Organizing

I'm a firm believer in the "broken windows theory," as discussed in Malcolm Gladwell's book *The Tipping Point*, which referenced an article published by social scientists James Wilson and George Kelling in 1982.

The point of this article is that the small cosmetic damages in a neighborhood can lead directly to large negative social issues. In other words, broken windows, trash on the street, and other cosmetic signs of urban blight lead to increased crime, antisocial behavior, and all sorts of other crimes.

What's funny is you can apply the broken windows theory to your daily life. By making small cosmetic changes to your routines, it's not hard to create an atmosphere that prevents a feeling of stress and overwhelm.

I feel the broken windows theory can be applied to your home and workspace. If you're surrounded by piles of clutter, it can have a negative impact on your mood or even your overall attitude toward the day.

So, even though "doing the dishes" isn't a life-altering habit, it's a small action that's both meditative and relaxing. In fact, usually while I'm doing the dishes, I'll think about the important tasks that I have to accomplish that day.

## Habit 5: Review My Quarterly Goals

Time required: Two minutes

Goal fulfilled: All (since I have a goal for each area of my life)

A daily goal review is important because it's a quick way to gauge whether my planned tasks for the day directly align with my plans for the next few months. This review acts as a reminder to stick with my goals, plus it helps me avoid any "shiny objects" that might become a distraction.

## Habit 6: Identify Three Priority Tasks in Todoist

Time required: Three minutes

Goal fulfilled: Career

It's easy to feel overwhelmed if you have dozens of planned tasks. That's why I like to start each day by working on the **three most important tasks**.

These activities have the biggest impact on my business, so I make sure to create a plan for completing them before anything else. When I've identified these priority items, I'll add them to the Todoist app and create a reminder that they are important. (For more on this, be sure to check out the Todoist tutorial that's part of the companion website.)

## Habit 7: Write in the Freedom Journal

Time required: Five minutes

Goal fulfilled: Career and spirituality

Journaling can have an amazing impact on your success. When you write down your thoughts, fears, and current challenges, you have a chance to gain clarity on what's truly important. It's a mindfulness habit that helps you make effective decisions on your daily actions. The tool that I prefer is The Freedom Journal.

The Freedom Journal was launched in 2016 by John Lee Dumas, a popular entrepreneur and podcaster. While journaling is completely optional to the learning process, I recommend it because it can help you focus on a single major goal and work at it for the next one hundred days. The journal will help you stay on track and make sure that you're hitting all the important milestones for your career.

## Habit 8: Review My Personal Capital Account

Time required: Two minutes

Goal fulfilled: Finance

Moving from journaling to this habit signifies the unofficial start of my "computer time" for the day. The first thing I always like to check is my Personal Capital account.

Personal Capital is a service that syncs all your investments, which tracks your growth and gives you an accurate "net worth" number. I like to review my account daily because it gives me a solid look at my current financial situation, which I can use to make small decisions about how I'm spending and where I'm investing my money.

## Habit 9: Analyze One Real Estate Investment Property

Time required: Five minutes

Goal fulfilled: Leisure and Finance

Real estate investing is a skill I'd like to master in the next five years. The one thing I've learned recently is you need to regularly analyze investment deals—even when you're not ready to make a purchase. This daily action prepares me for those occasional moments when I see a good property and need to take immediate action.

This small action is straightforward. Each day, I load my preferred website to find investment properties and then analyze the numbers of one deal. This means calculating the purchase price, how much the tenant is currently paying, property taxes, and home insurance. Almost always, this "back-of-the-napkin math" tells me that a property isn't the right fit. But every few weeks, I'll come across a hidden gem that might be worth pursuing.

## Habit 10: Manage Book Marketing Campaigns

Time required: > Five minutes

Goal fulfilled: Career

The second-to-last habit is also the most time-consuming. It's also the point where I make the transition from morning routine into "work mode." At this point, I'll go to three sites that are used to promote my books: BookBub Ads, Amazon Marketing Services, and Amazon Associates.

The goal here is to track the success of the previous day's book marketing campaigns and then make small adjustments to improve my return on investment (ROI).

Since this habit requires a technical explanation, I'll keep it simple by saying that this habit is completed by punching numbers into an Excel spreadsheet, then comparing how much money I've spent on a campaign versus how much I've earned.

If I see a positive ROI (i.e., the campaign is profitable), then I'll increase its expenditures. But if I see a negative ROI, then I'll either tweak the ad or pause the entire campaign.

This small habit is probably one of my most important because it helps me scale my author business by reaching new readers. Like many of the strategies discussed throughout this book, it's often the littlest actions that have the biggest impact on your career and personal life.

## Habit 11: Prepare a Smoothie Drink

Time required: Five minutes

Goal fulfilled: Health

We've all heard about the benefits of juicing and starting your day with a powerful shake, but sometimes it's a hard habit to remember. So, the last thing I do before diving into work is to grab a bunch of ingredients, throw them into my Nutribullet, and then prepare a delicious smoothie that I'll drink during the first few minutes of my workday.

I often mix up different recipes, but I like to make ones that include proteins, fruits, vegetables, potassium, and antioxidants. Really, my choice in a smoothie depends on my mood that day and what ingredients are available. (If you're interested in seeing some of the ones that I typically drink, you can check out the NutriLiving website and app, which are part of the NutriBullet brand.)

## End with a Keystone Habit

We've talked about the importance of "keystone habits," which are any action that has a positive impact on multiple areas of your life. The reason I'm mentioning it again is I always like to complete my habit stacking routine by immediately diving into my top keystone habit—*writing*.

Writing helps me clear my mind (spirituality), generate income (career), and reduce stress (health). So I prefer to start the day with this habit because I can harness the energetic state generated from the habit stacking routine and then use it to start my most important task with a bang!

Now, writing is how I prefer to start the day. You, on the other hand, might want to focus on something different. The point here is that when you complete a habit stacking routine, you can build "emotional momentum" that has a positive spillover effect on your next few actions. My advice is to pick the one keystone habit that has the biggest impact on your life.

Well, that's my routine. Now let's shift gears and start talking about you. In the next section, I'll dive into the simple rules for building your first stacks.

# 9 Rules to Build a Habit Stacking Routine

It's easy to get confused about *how* to build a habit stacking routine. In fact, you might think it's a series of random activities thrown together in a haphazard manner. That can't be further from the truth!

When creating a stack, you want to consider a few important elements: Why are you choosing each action? What order should they go in? And how long do you spend on each activity?

To keep things simple, I recommend using the following nine rules to build your habit stacks.

## 1. Attach the stack to an existing habit.

The simplest way to remember a stack is to do it right before or after a habit. This should be something you do without fail, every single day—like eating, brushing your teeth, or checking your phone. This is important because you're going to piggyback on this habit by creating what's called an "if-then plan."

If-then plans (also known as implementation intentions) can help you stick with a goal and, more importantly, will prevent those times when you want to skip a day. The idea here is to identify an existing habit then create a plan for the specific action you'll complete immediately before *or* after this routine.

For instance, you could create if-then plans like:

> » "I will start my habit stacking routine right after I walk into the living room first thing in the morning."

» "I will floss my teeth right before I brush them in the evening."

» "I will give 'one last look' before turning left while driving." (This one action saved my life a few months back.)

» "I will pack my gym bag right after I put on my clothes for the day."

» "I will eat a salad right before my dinner."

As you can see, each if-then plan is attached to an existing behavior. So, once you create an if-then plan, all you need to do is add a reminder to make sure it's completed.

## 2. Complete each habit in five minutes or less (usually).

Let me start by saying that the five-minute rule *isn't* written in stone. Instead, use it as a general rule of thumb. So, if you feel that one habit is important, but it takes longer than five minutes, then it's okay to add it to your daily stack.

Just remember this: you only have a limited amount of time to work on self-improvement, which for most people is a daily average of thirty minutes. This means it's easy to complete ten habits that average three minutes of effort. But it also means you can't complete too many small actions if each requires ten minutes of effort.

I recommend five minutes because it's a basic unit of time in which you can accomplish a surprising number of things, while being short enough that you can stack each action on top of another. Five minutes is 0.35% of your day. Just one-third of one percent of your day will help you create a habit that results in long-term change and benefits.

That said, if a specific action takes *slightly* longer than five minutes, then it's perfectly okay to add it to your routine. If it's important to you, then you should make it part of your daily activity.

## 3. The entire routine should take under thirty minutes.

The "thirty-minute rule" is a sweet spot where you can complete many habits without it interfering with everything else in your life. But if you're super busy, then it's okay to do twenty-, fifteen-, ten-, or even five-minute stacks. Again, the most important thing to remember here is consistency.

You'd be surprised at many "little things" can be squeezed into a half hours' time. In fact, when you get to Part V of the book, you'll discover a large assortment of important habits that can fit into anyone's busy schedule.

## 4. Build daily, weekly, and monthly stacks.

Some habits don't require daily effort. Instead, they are best completed on a weekly or monthly interval. For instance, certain actions only require the occasional "checkup," like reviewing your credit card purchases, inspecting your smoke detectors, and checking your tire pressure. Each is important, but it's better to schedule these actions on a weekly or monthly basis.

My advice is simple: not only should you build daily stacks, but you should also schedule time once a week and once a month to complete those important but not urgent activities.

For the weekly review, you could schedule this activity late Sunday night as a way to prepare for the workweek. And for the monthly review, you could schedule it for the first Saturday of each month. But it really doesn't matter when these activities are scheduled. The important thing is to put these stacks into your calendar so you'll follow up on them.

## 5. Each small habit should be a complete action.

There should be an obvious starting and stopping point. In other words, you should avoid habits where you could easily do more of it if you had time (like exercising, writing, or anything related to your job). It's better to schedule these activities for a different part of the day when you can devote more time.

For instance, there isn't a lot of value in cramming five minutes of exercise into a stack because it won't give you the full benefit of improved fitness and strength. Instead, a better use of your time is to pack your gym bag for the day or record a workout from the day before. Each action supports your larger keystone habits and has a clear starting and stopping point.

**There is one major exception to this rule.** You could add the occasional "elephant habit" to your daily stack to make forward progress on an unpleasant task. By chipping away at this project in small five- to ten-minute increments, you won't procrastinate on the tasks that you know need to get done but aren't very fun.

## 6. Pick simple-to-complete activities.

Each small action should be easy to complete without requiring a lot of brainpower. The idea here is to do it quickly and then immediately move on to the next action. If you need time to complete a series of steps, then perhaps you should schedule this habit for another time in the day.

Remember, each activity should only require a single step, or maybe two steps, to complete. Examples include making a bed, packing a bag, preparing a smoothie, or updating your expenditures from the previous day.

## 7. Map out a logical progression for each routine.

The entire routine should flow like a well-oiled machine. This is key because you want to avoid wasting time and moving from room to room.

For instance, let's pretend you complete two actions in your bedroom, three in the kitchen, and two in your office. It would be a mistake to put these habits into an order where you're running back and forth between rooms. Instead, schedule them in a logical flow that matches the normal actions you complete with your existing routines.

Just think back to my eleven habits from the previous section. Almost all the habits are completed in a logical progression where I move from the bathroom into the kitchen, then to the dining room, and finally to my office. There is no wasted effort because each action is anchored to a specific spot in the house.

## 8. Use a checklist to manage the process.

A stack isn't made up on the spot. It should be a set of actions that *you* determine ahead of time that are personally important. This means putting each habit into a step-by-step checklist that you'll refer to constantly.

This checklist should be a set of actions done the same way, in the same order each day.

Sure, it's okay to add *or* delete certain habits if they don't work for you. But the only way to stick with this routine is to turn it into automatic behavior. In fact, when you do it often enough, you'll complete these actions without consciously thinking about why you're doing them. You'll simply act on autopilot.

Where this checklist is stored is up to you. There are a variety of places where you can keep this list, like:

- » A journal or notebook
- » Todoist
- » Evernote
- » Wunderlist
- » Remember the Milk

The choices are practically infinite here. There are hundreds of different tools you can use to store this checklist. Just pick one and stick with it!

Never underestimate the power of checklists. Not only do they help people stay organized, but they also save lives. For more on this, I highly recommend *The Checklist Manifesto* by Atul Gawande, which talks about how simple checklists have been proven to save lives in the airline and medical industries.

## 9. Include habits that relate to your priorities.

Remember, the benefit of habit stacking is to take action on your important, personal goals. These should be outcomes *you* want to achieve—not what others want from you. In fact, at no point should you feel like you "must" do a specific habit. Instead, each task should have a clearly identifiable benefit that you're seeking.

The simplest way to identify habits is to make sure they relate to a goal from one of these seven areas:

1. Career
2. Finance
3. Health
4. Leisure
5. Organizing
6. Relationships
7. Spirituality

The choice here is yours.

It's a "choose your own adventure" decision where you pick habits that you want to build. (And, as a reminder, if you do get stuck, we have the 127 ideas that start in Part V of the book.)

All that said, I recommend using this rule of thumb before picking any habit that goes into a stack:

**"Know your 'reason why' you're completing this habit."**

If you can't identify a clear benefit of an activity, then it shouldn't go in the routine.

Okay, you now know the rules for building a stack, so let's shift focus and discuss the *how-to* part of the process. Specifically, I'll detail the thirteen-step process for building a habit stacking routine.

# 13 Steps for Building a Habit Stacking Routine

**The key to consistency is to treat a habit stack like a single action instead of a series of individual tasks.** I know this seems like a small thing, but building a habit requires many elements if you want it to stick, like: 1. Scheduling time for activity (a block of time). 2. Identifying a trigger. 3. Planning what you'll do to complete the action. So on and so forth.

My point here?

If you treated each component of a stack as an individual action, then you'd have to create a reminder and track each behavior, which can quickly become overwhelming. However, if you treat the entire routine as just one habit, then it will be easier to remember and complete on a consistent basis.

Habit stacking can feel overwhelming at first. However, once you get started and do it a few times, it's not as hard as you think.

The key to success here is to start with small expectations, build the muscle memory of completing this routine, and then add more tasks once you're consistent. In this section, you'll learn how to do all of this.

What you're about to discover is a proven thirteen-step process for building a permanent habit stack. It's a straightforward process that won't leave you feeling overwhelmed. If you closely follow (and complete) these steps, you'll discover it's easy to create lasting change in your life. (And if you want a downloadable easy-to-follow version of this process, then be sure to grab a copy on the companion website.)

Let's get to it.

## Step 1: Start with a Five-Minute Block

The simplest way to stick with a new habit is to make it "stupidly simple" to complete, which is a valuable lesson that I learned from *Mini Habits* by Stephen Guise.

As an example, if you want to write every day, then you create a goal of writing just one paragraph per day. Sure, you can do more than that, but as long as you've written this paragraph, then you can consider this a complete task for the day. The core idea is to set a simple goal that overcomes inertia. Then usually, once you get started, you'll do more of the task then you originally planned.

I recommend applying the mini-habits strategy to your stacks. At first, the most important factor is consistency. That's why you should **start with five minutes, picking one or two habits**, and then add more as this routine becomes an automatic action.

Don't think this is enough time to accomplish anything?

Well, if you review the chapter that details my eleven-habit stack, then you'll discover four habits that took a total five minutes to complete. Not bad for a condensed block of time, right?

Furthermore, there are dozens of habits starting in Part V that only take a minute or two. So, even though a five-minute block might not seem like a lot, you'd be amazed at how much activity can be compressed into this short amount of time.

## Step 2: Focus on Small Wins

Build your routine around habits that don't require a lot of effort. These are the small wins that will build "emotional momentum" because they're easy to remember and complete.

When I say small wins, I mean actions that require little willpower, like taking a vitamin, weighing yourself, filling a thirty-two-ounce bottle of water, or reviewing your goals.

Yes, they are incredibly easy tasks, but that's the point here. You want to get started with these "no-brainer" activities because they will eliminate the likelihood that you'll skip a day due to a feeling of overwhelm or general busyness.

To complete this step, look at the seven goal categories in Part II. Find actions that are easy to complete—like anything under two minutes. Then build your stack around these simple actions.

Focus on these activities for a week or two until this stack is automatic. *Only then* should you add more habits to this routine.

## Step 3: Pick a Time and Location

**Every stack should be anchored to a trigger related to a location, time of day, or combination of both**. Here are a few examples that can be used to act as prompts to complete a specific stack.

*At home, in the morning:* Completing a routine first thing in the morning is a great way to start the day in an energized state. You can complete a series of habits that have a positive benefit to your life, which will carry over into the important tasks that start your workday.

The small habits could include meditating, reviewing your goals, reciting affirmations, reading a nonfiction book, or drinking a nutritious shake.

*At work, in the morning:* You just got to the office, so instead of checking your email or social media (like most people do), maximize the first few hours by creating an environment that allows you to focus on your high-level tasks.

The small habits could include identifying three priority tasks for the day, picking the "next steps" for your top projects, removing distractions, and starting your day by working on the hardest task.

*At work, on your lunch break:* The middle of the day is a great time to complete a stack. You've just worked for a few hours, so you'll probably feel a decrease in energy. A great way to overcome this negative state is to eat a quick lunch at your desk (before or after the stack) and then complete habits that prepare you for the rest of the day.

The small habits could include meditating, taking a brisk walk, getting in a seven-minute workout, calling an accountability partner, or completing a "deskercise" routine.

*At work, at the end of the workday:* The last few minutes at work are the perfect time to complete a stack because it'll set you up for success when you come back the next morning (or after the weekend). You've been busy all day, so having an end-of-the-day routine will leave you feeling positive about all you've accomplished.

The small habits could include writing in a journal, identifying the important tasks for the next day, or tracking the amount of time you spent on each activity.

*At home, early in the evening:* You can also squeeze in a stack between when you get home and when you go to bed. In fact, this is the perfect opportunity to work on those small, personal projects that are important but never seem to be urgent enough to demand your attention.

The small habits could include practicing a skill, planning meals for the week, reviewing your expenditures, or organizing a small section of your home.

*At the gym (or wherever you exercise):* Yes, you can add a stack to an exercise routine. In fact, creating a routine for your workout will help you complete the important exercises in the shortest amount of time.

While exercising isn't part of a stack, there are many support habits that will help you stick this activity. These include stretching, drinking a healthy smoothie, weighing yourself, recording the metrics from your workout stats, or creating a playlist full of your favorite music or podcasts.

## Step 4: Anchor Your Stack to a Trigger

The word "trigger" has a different meaning for many people. *My* definition of a trigger is a cue that uses one of your five senses (sight, sound, smell, touch, or taste), which acts as a reminder to complete a specific action.

Triggers are important because most people can't remember a large number of tasks without a reminder. So, a trigger can push you into taking action. For instance, many people use their alarm clocks or cell phones as a trigger to wake them up in the morning.

**There are two basic types of triggers**. The first are *external triggers* (like a cell phone alarm, a push notification, or a Post-it note on your refrigerator). External triggers work because they create a Pavlovian response that when the alarm goes off, you complete a specific task.

The second type are *internal triggers*, which are the feelings, thoughts, and emotions that you relate to an established habit. These are like a scratch that you must itch.

For instance, if you've ever compulsively felt the need to "check in" with social media, then this action was the direct result of an internal trigger.

It's important to understand the difference between these two triggers—not only because it'll help you build powerful habit stacks, but also because it will help you overcome bad habits that might be limiting your personal growth.

Let me explain.

### Triggers (a Negative Example)

As you know, there are many popular social media sites like Facebook, Twitter, Instagram, and Pinterest. Love or hate them, these sites have become a ubiquitous part of our modern culture.

But how did they become so popular?

The companies that created them understand how the human mind works, so they've designed their systems to "hook" users into coming back for more.

If you've ever used a social site, then you've probably noticed it uses alerts for all sorts of behaviors. Whenever someone comments, likes, shares, Tweets, or re-pins something you've posted, you get a notification. These cues are visual or auditory cues—or both. A signal goes off, and you respond—like one of Pavlov's dogs.

These triggers can be addictive because they act as a "reward" for posting content that people appreciate. In fact, at some point, you've probably logged into a social site *just* to see what others think about an update you've posted.

The repeated exposure of notifications creates a habit loop that Charles Duhigg discusses in the book *The Power of Habit*, which breaks down into three actions:

1. Cue: The visual or auditory reminder to use the social site.
2. Routine: The pattern you follow to check in (e.g., open the app or click to the website).
3. Reward: The psychological benefit you receive by using the social site (e.g., someone likes or shares your post).

I feel these triggers can be *negative* when they create a permanent behavior where you feel a compulsive need to check a site multiple times each day. In fact, without being prompted (like when you feel bored), you'll often feel an unconscious desire to go to a social site without even knowing why you're doing it.

This is a classic example of an internal trigger. Through repeated exposure to a social site, you create a permanent habit. Whenever you feel bored or distracted, you can get a quick dopamine rush by checking your favorite social media site. And what usually happens is the "few minutes" you thought you'd be on the site turns into thirty or more minutes of wasted time.

Technology companies use external triggers all the time to create these compulsive internal triggers. It's how they build "loyal" customers. They know that repeated exposure to an external cue will increase overall usage—especially if the product provides an escape from an otherwise boring day. Eventually, users will access their product whenever they feel unmotivated.

So, if a product provides a positive benefit (e.g., a budgeting app like Mint), then it's programmed to build good habits. But if a product can be harmful (e.g., an addictive video game like Trivia Crack), then it's programmed to build bad habits.

For more on this topic, I recommend the book *Hooked* by Nir Eyal, which goes into a lengthy explanation of how technology is designed to encourage addictive behaviors, and what you can do to recognize these patterns in your life (and hopefully remove them).

Now, if you'll forgive my minor rant against social media, I do think there is something valuable to be learned by understanding triggers. In fact, you can use this knowledge to build positive habits into your life. So, let's talk about that next.

**Triggers (a Positive Example)**

My recommendation is to create a trigger for each habit stacking routine. One example of this is to put dental floss in an obvious location on your bathroom counter, next to your toothbrush. This will act as a visual reminder to floss, either before or after you brush your teeth.

That's just one example of a trigger. If you want to create triggers for your stacks, then I recommend keeping four things in mind:

1. **A trigger should be an existing habit.** This is an action you do automatically *every* day, like showering, brushing your teeth, checking your phone, going to the refrigerator, or sitting down at your desk. This is important because you need to be 100% certain that you won't miss a reminder.

2. **A trigger can be a specific time of day.** The reminder for a habit can also happen at a specific time each day, like waking up in the morning, eating lunch, or walking through the door after work. Again, whatever you choose should be an automatic behavior.

3. **A trigger should be easy to complete.** If an action is challenging (even if it's something you do daily), then you decrease the effectiveness of the trigger. For instance, even if you exercise regularly, it's a mistake to use it as a trigger because you might occasionally miss a day.

4. **A trigger shouldn't be a new habit.** It takes anywhere from twenty-one to sixty-six days to create a permanent habit. Sometimes it's even longer for the ones that are really challenging. So, you shouldn't pick a new habit as a trigger because you're not 100% certain that it'll become a consistent action.

Those are just a few rules of thumb for picking a trigger. To simplify it even further, I recommend picking any of the following habits because you probably already do them daily:

- » Eating breakfast
- » Eating lunch
- » Eating dinner
- » Brushing your teeth

» Getting into your car before work

» Walking into your house after work

» Arriving (or leaving) your place of employment

» Opening/starting your computer in the morning

» Setting a mobile phone alarm at a specific time

» Keeping a visual reminder in a key location, like your computer, refrigerator, or television

As you can see, there are many types of triggers that can act as reminders for your stack. Really, the easiest way to pick one is to *match the trigger to the first habit of the routine.* The goal here is to create a trigger that prompts you into action, and then you'll use the checklist to guide you through the rest of the small actions. So, let's talk about that next.

## Step 5: Create a Logical Checklist

The checklist is the most important part of a stack. It should include the sequence of the actions, how long it takes to complete each one, and where you'll do them. I'll admit it's a little obsessive to include all this information, but it will remove any guesswork about what you need to do to complete a specific action.

We have already talked about checklists, so I won't waste time rehashing the same material. Suffice to say, you should put the small actions together in a way that they seamlessly flow into each other without wasted effort.

## Step 6: Be Accountable

You've probably heard about the law of inertia (also known as Newton's First Law of Motion). If not, the law states that "an object at rest stays at rest and an object in motion stays in motion with the same speed and in the same direction unless acted upon by an unbalanced force."

In other words, if your natural tendency is to lounge around before starting the day, then you'll need an extra "push" to force you into action. People often fail at building habits because it's easier to stay resting than it is to do something new and potentially unpleasant.

In fact, one of the biggest lessons I've learned about habit development is that **you need *accountability* to stick to a major goal**.

It's not enough to make a personal commitment. The big things in life require a solid action plan and a support network to tap into whenever you encounter an obstacle. This is true in the business world *and* for your personal development. When you have someone to cheer on your successes (or kick you in the butt when you're slacking), you're less likely to give up.

There are a variety of ways to be accountable, like posting your progress on social media accounts, telling the people in your life about your new routine, or even "punishing" yourself for not staying committed to a goal by using an app like Beeminder.

There are two techniques that have personally worked for me when trying to build a new habit:

The first is Coach.me, which is a great tool for maintaining and sticking to new habits. It's like having a coach in your pocket, both for better and worse. You'll be held accountable for your habit stacking routine by adding it as a habit and checking in every single day when it's been completed. Trust me—the simple act of knowing that you have to update people on your progress is motivation enough to stick to a habit stacking routine.

The second is having an accountability partner with whom you share your breakthroughs, challenges, and future plans. This is a great way to get a kick in the butt whenever you feel a wane in motivation, and someone you can confide in whenever you have a challenge that requires a second opinion.

If you're interested in finding prospective accountability partners, then be sure to check out my Facebook group, HabitsGroup.com, which has over 1,000 members. Every month we create a thread where members can connect with one another and become accountability partners.

## Step 7: Create Small, Enjoyable Rewards

Completing your habit stacking routine is an accomplishment, and it should be rewarded as such.

Giving yourself a reward can be a great motivator to complete a daily routine. This can include anything, like watching your favorite TV show, eating a healthy snack, or even relaxing for a few minutes.

Really, a reward can be anything that you frequently enjoy. My only piece of advice is to avoid any reward that eliminates the benefit of a specific habit. So if you've just completed small actions to lose weight, then your reward shouldn't be a 400-calorie cupcake. It defeats the purpose of the stack, doesn't it?

If you'd like more ideas, then I encourage you to read one of my blog posts, which covers 155 ways to reward yourself.

## Step 8: Focus on Repetition

Repetition is key for the first few weeks when building a stack. It's crucial that you stick to the routine—even if you must skip one or two small actions. Consistency is more important than anything else. Repetition builds muscle memory. And when you complete the routine often enough, it'll become an ingrained part of your day, like brushing your teeth.

All that said, **it's not the end of the world if you miss the occasional day**. It happens to the best of us. But you must never, *ever* miss two days in a row. This will create a slippery slope where it'll become progressively easier to miss future days. Do this often enough and you'll probably give up on the routine. This leads us to another piece of advice ...

## Step 9: Don't Break the Chain

One of the most interesting habit-related stories I've ever heard comes from the popular comedian Jerry Seinfeld. When talking to a budding comedian, Seinfeld gave a simple piece of advice: Set aside time *every day* to create new material. The key here is to never miss a day, even if you're not in the mood. (Sounds like familiar advice, right?)

At the start of every year, Seinfeld hangs a one-year calendar on his wall and makes a big red X on the calendar for every day he writes new comedy material. He doesn't have to write a lot of material every day. What's important is to do something every single day, without fail. His focus is to *never break the chain.*

Marking X's on a calendar encourages you to complete your desired task every single day. The more you look at an unbroken string of red X's, the more compulsion you'll feel to get over any initial resistance and force yourself to get started.

The purpose of not breaking the chain is to eliminate your excuses. Sometimes it's easy to think of creative reasons not to get started with a stack. You're tired, busy, overwhelmed, sick, hung over, or depressed. All of these can be valid reasons to skip a routine. But if you regularly miss a day, then you'll make it even easier to skip another day whenever you don't feel like doing the list.

My advice is simple: Create a doable daily goal that can be achieved no matter what happens, and don't let yourself be talked out of it. Perhaps you'll set a small goal where you only complete two or three actions. The important thing is to set a goal that can be achieved even when you have an off day.

## Step 10: Expect Setbacks

Even the most consistent habits will experience the occasional setback or challenge. In fact, when you've done something long enough, I guarantee there will be times when you experience an unexpected setback.

For instance, I have been a runner since 1990. Do the math and you'll see that's **twenty-seven years** of distance running. In the almost thirty years of this exercise habit, I have experienced a variety of setbacks, such as boredom, multiple injuries, weird illnesses (scarlet fever and pericarditis were two of my favorites), dog attacks, life-threating car incidents, and life-threatening *pedestrian* incidents.

As you can imagine, these various incidents have made life interesting when it comes to staying consistent with this one habit. But it's also taught me the importance of resilience and sticking with something *even* when you experience a setback.

I'd actually go as far as saying that **setbacks are good things**. They teach you resiliency and help you become *Antifragile*, as Nassim Nicholas Taleb discusses in his book by the same name.

The bottom line is you should expect challenges to come up with this routine. When they do, you have one of two choices: give up or find a way to overcome them. Hopefully you'll look for ways to overcome these obstacles. If so, then I recommend checking out Part XII whenever you encounter an obstacle.

## Step 11: Schedule the Frequency of a Stack

As we've discussed before, some stacks only need to be completed on an irregular basis:

1. Daily
2. Weekly
3. Monthly

At first, you should get started with a small daily habit stack. But as you become comfortable with the strategy, I'd recommend creating a stack for each of the above three times.

Ideally, these stacks should be "check-in habits" that you know are important but are easy to forget, like reviewing your credit card statements, completing safety checks, and planning fun activities. By putting them into a routinely scheduled activity, you'll make sure these tasks get completed without them weighing on your subconscious as yet another project that you haven't finished.

## Step 12: Scale up Your Stack

Think back to the first step of this process: "Start with a five-minute block." If you can devote only a limited amount of time to a stack, then you won't get much value from it. That's why I recommend you eventually build up to a thirty-minute routine, where you complete *at least* six small habits.

Do this in an incremental manner. In the first week, your routine will last five minutes. The second week will be ten minutes, then up fifteen minutes for week three. Repeat this process until the routine is thirty minutes with a handful of small actions.

Now, this scaling up doesn't mean you'll haphazardly add a bunch of small habits. Instead, you should make sure you're consistently completing the routine and not experiencing resistance to this activity.

Don't ignore any feelings of stress, boredom, or overwhelm when it comes to your stacks. If you notice that it's getting progressively harder to get started (e.g., you're procrastinating), then you should either reduce the number of habits or start asking yourself *why* you want to skip a day. The more you understand about your lack of motivation, the easier it will be to overcome it.

## Step 13: Build One Routine at a Time

One of the biggest debates around is how long it takes to build a permanent habit. Some people say it's twenty-one days, and others say it's a few months. In fact, in a study published in the European Journal of Social Psychology, Phillippa Lally found that it takes anywhere from 18 to 254 days for an action to become a permanent habit, with the average being 66 days.

**The lesson here is you shouldn't try to build more than one habit at a time because each additional new action will make it increasingly difficult to stick with your stacks.**

Really, the only time I even consider adding a new stack is when I stop thinking of a habit as a habit. Instead, it's simply "what I do" every day without any thought of *why* or *how* I'm completing these actions.

When *you* feel that a stack has become a permanent behavior, that is when you can add a new habit to your daily routine. There isn't a specific recommended timeline. Instead, the answer will be different from person to person.

## Putting It All Together

There you have it: **thirteen steps to build a habit stacking routine**.

If you follow this blueprint, you can identify those important small actions, put them into a logical framework, and then complete each one with a single trigger or cue.

At this point, you fully understand why habit stacking is beneficial and how to make it part of your day. But you might have a few final questions about this routine. So, let's go over them. After that, we'll get to the 127 small actions you can use to create the perfect stack.

# 4 Questions about Habit Stacking

As you can see from the previous example, it's not hard to squeeze almost a dozen habits into a thirty-minute block of time. In fact, you can use this routine to benefit many areas of your life: health, finances, career, and spirituality, just to name a few. I truly feel if you're looking for a simple way to add small actions into your day, then habit stacking can help you do it.

That said, I've received a few questions about this process over the past few years, so I want to briefly answer them before diving into the specific habits you can build.

## Question #1: "Do you always do every item on this list?"

No.

Sometimes, if I feel a specific habit isn't important for that day (like managing a book marketing campaign), then I'll skip it. Really, that's the beauty of habit stacking. You can pick and choose the actions based on your current goals and schedule. The only important thing is to be consistent.

## Question #2: "Aren't some of these habits common sense?"

Yes.

I'm probably not the first person who has told you to drink more water, so I won't pretend it's a revolutionary piece of advice. That said, while everyone knows drinking water is important, they'll often fail to create a system in their lives to help them **follow through** on these important actions.

With habit stacking, you no longer wonder when (or how) you'll drink more water, because it will become a scheduled action that doesn't require a lot of effort or brainpower. You simply make it part of a routine (with other "common sense habits") and schedule time when you can get them done!

### Question #3: "Do you also complete important habits recommended by others, like reading, meditating, and exercising?"

Yes.

Again, there are common sense habits that everyone knows are important, like reading, meditating, and exercising. However, there are two reasons why they are not included in my morning stack:

1. Each takes longer to complete than five minutes, so I like to schedule them for later in my day.
2. Each of those habit helps me relax, so I like to do them after completing hard tasks.

Remember: habit stacking is about making decisions that are right for *your* situation. You're the ultimate decision maker of what goes into a routine and what doesn't make the cut.

### Question #4: "Isn't this a robotic way to live your life?"

No.

Well, actually, it might feel that way at first.

When you begin a new stack, you must rely on a checklist to remember each action because there is a finite amount of information that can be stored in your short-term memory. While you might feel silly moving from habit to habit using a checklist, you'll eventually reach the point where each action becomes second nature. They will transition from "habit stacking routine" into a series of positive actions you complete each day, like flossing your teeth and eating healthy foods.

# About the 127 Small Actions Covered in This Book

Well, we've now arrived at the 127 small actions that were promised at the beginning of the book. I recognize that 17,000 words is a lot of content to go through to "get to the good stuff." However, I feel this information was necessary because I don't want you to look at these small actions and think of them as obvious suggestions.

**Remember:** The value of habit stacking doesn't come from the individual actions. Most of us already know *how* we can improve our lives. What we *don't know* is the process for taking all these small suggestions and turning them into a simple-to-follow framework.

So, I want to give you a challenge here ...

Instead of simply reading the following list, look for small habits that resonate with your life. If you feel that a few actions might benefit you, then highlight or bookmark them for future reference. This will become important when you implement this information and start building your own stacks.

The following sections are broken down according to the seven primary areas of your life:

1. Career
2. Finance
3. Health
4. Leisure
5. Organizing
6. Relationship

7.  Spirituality

You could pick one or two habits from each category to have a well-rounded stack, or you could focus on one specific category (like completing a series of habits to improve your career). As always, the choice is yours. This is a choose-your-own-adventure book where the habits you pick are the ones that you feel are personally important.

Finally, each small action is broken down into five components:

1.  **Type:** Is it a keystone, support, or elephant habit? (Review Part II if you're confused about the difference between the three.)

2.  **Best time to complete:** When should you complete this action? This isn't written in stone, but I feel some habits are best done at a specific point in the day.

3.  **Frequency:** How often should you complete this habit? Daily? Weekly? Monthly?

4.  **Description:** What actions do you need to take to complete this habit?

5.  **Benefit:** In what way does this habit benefit the specific category of your life?

Throughout this list, you'll find habits that you probably know are important. But I guarantee you'll discover a few that you've never considered before. We have a lot of ground to cover here, so let's dive right in with the career habits.

# PART V

## CAREER HABITS (#1 to #20)

Focusing on career habits has many benefits: you can increase productivity, improve job performance, and get more from each day to positively impact other areas of your life.

Most habits in this section focus on productivity, which is simply a measure of your work efficiency during any given day. I've also included a number of small actions that will streamline your professional life. If you add any of the following to a stack, you'll see a dramatic improvement in both the quantity *and* the quality of your workday efforts.

Let's get to it.

### #1. Schedule Your Day

**Type:** Keystone habit

**Best time to complete:** Morning

**Frequency:** Daily

**Benefit:** Without a schedule, it's frighteningly easy to get to the end of the day and realize you've achieved nothing of importance. At the very least, you should make a list of the tasks you want to accomplish during the day and decide where your priorities lie.

This small habit is perfect for someone who has to work on many tasks and *can't* narrow down this list to the **three most important tasks** (which we'll talk about next).

**Description:** Make a list of the tasks you want to complete by the end of the day. Try to be realistic about your efficiency instead of creating a lengthy list of tasks that will be impossible to complete.

Use the Eisenhower Decision Matrix to rate the importance of each task: 1 (important and urgent), 2 (important, but not urgent), 3 (not important, but urgent), or 4 (not important, not urgent).

Structure your day so you work on the first-quadrant tasks, then the second, then the third, and finally only work on the fourth if you have time (or if you want to goof off by completing a mindless task).

Schedule each task at a specific time, and be sure to include breaks. If you feel restricted by a tight schedule, then you can split your tasks into morning and afternoon sessions instead. The crucial thing here is to make sure that your day is focused on the activities that bring the most value to your job or business.

## #2. Identify Your Three Most Important Tasks (MITs)

**Type:** Keystone habit

**Best time to complete:** Morning

**Frequency:** Daily

**Benefit:** Another way to structure your day is to focus on your most important tasks (MITs) before anything else. This eliminates the problem of scheduling too many activities, and the feeling of failure when you don't accomplish them all.

Identifying three MITs ahead of time keeps you focused on priority activities. In fact, if you *only* complete the MITs, then you can still consider it a productive day.

**Description:** If you keep a list of your projects in an app (like Todoist or Evernote), then it's easy to identify your next tasks. From this list, pick the three tasks that have the highest priority or are considered both urgent and important. Don't work on anything else until you have completed these MITs.

## #3. Review Your Goals

**Type:** Keystone habit

**Best time to complete:** Mornings

**Frequency:** Daily

**Benefit:** Everybody has goals. Sadly, the hustle and bustle of life often derails us from what we'd like to accomplish. That's why it's important to review goals daily, so you can create a plan of what you need to do *that day* to make progress on these outcomes.

Goals can be set for the day, week, month, quarter, or year. My rule of thumb is to create five to seven goals per quarter (i.e., every three months), and I recommend you do the same. Quarterly goals are far enough away so that you can achieve significant outcomes. But it's also a short enough period that you can adjust if your long-term plans change.

**Description:** Keep your goals in an easy-to-access place. This could be in a binder or an app like Evernote. Then, once or twice a day, take five minutes to review these goals.

During this review, read each goal aloud and think about the tasks you have scheduled for that day. For each item, ask yourself, "How does this action bring me closer to one of my goals?" If you can't come up with a good answer, then perhaps it's a task that you should be skipped or delegated.

## #4. Do the Hardest Task First

**Type:** Support habit

**Best time to complete:** Anytime

**Frequency:** Daily

**Benefit:** When you look at your list of tasks, it's tempting to choose the smaller, easier tasks to do first. If you have a big project that fills you with dread, you're much more likely to procrastinate and put it off until later. However, if you do that task first, you'll feel energized knowing that the toughest item has been crossed off your list. The result is that all other tasks will feel like a breeze in comparison.

A study of elite musicians found that rather than practicing more than their peers, they were instead engaging in more deliberate practice, focusing on their hardest tasks and being more productive during their practice sessions. If you look at the hardest task on your list, you'll probably find that it is also the task that will give you the most benefit.

**Description:** Look at your list of MITs and underline the one that you know you'd put off indefinitely if you had the chance. Get started on this task before you have a chance to think about it. Don't work on your other tasks until it's finished.

## #5. Chunk Down a Project (or Task) into Manageable Steps

**Type:** Support habit

**Best time to complete:** Morning

**Frequency:** Daily

**Benefit:** Sometimes a project is so overwhelming that you simply don't know where to get started. This leads to procrastination and unnecessary stress. But if you set aside time during a stack to create a step-by-step plan, you can improve your productivity because you'll know where to get started.

**Description:** For each of your major projects, take a few minutes to chunk it down into simple-to-complete steps. For instance, if one of your tasks is "write an article for my website," you could break it down like this:

1. Write the title, so you know what will be discussed.
2. Conduct research to find quality resources and good quotes.
3. Map out the subheadings and major talking points.
4. Write the first draft.
5. Write the second draft and tighten the copy.
6. Review with the third draft, checking spelling and grammar.
7. Format the post for your website.
8. Source and resize images.
9. Insert images.
10. Upload and schedule the article.

By breaking a task into specific actions, you'll have a better understanding of what needs to be done and how to schedule the work into your day.

## #6. Remove Distractions before Working

**Type:** Support habit

**Best time to complete:** Morning

**Frequency:** Daily

**Benefit:** Most people find it's impossible to ignore their email and social media notifications when trying to work. This means that if you're interrupted every few minutes by a ping, push notification, or text alert, then your productivity will be greatly reduced.

Yes, these social activities are pleasurable—they give our brains a little hit of dopamine, otherwise known as the happy hormone. In other words, social media can be addictive. A quick five minutes on Facebook can easily turn into an hour, as many of us can attest to.

Rather than struggling against your brain's natural inclination to procrastinate, save yourself a lot of time and hassle by simply closing your email tab and banning social media during work time.

**Description:** If you have strong willpower, then simply close out any app or website that might be distracting before a work session. However, if you're someone who can't rely on willpower alone, then there are a wide range of tools that can block your access to the most tempting distractions.

Here are a few apps and websites you can use:

- » Rescue Time: Understand how you spend your time so you can focus and increase your productivity.
- » StayFocusd: Limit the amount of time you spend on distracting websites by installing StayFocusd on your computer.
- » Cold Turkey: Similar to StayFocusd, Cold Turkey temporarily blocks distracting websites so you can focus on work.
- » SelfControl: Block out distracting websites for a set amount of time.

» Freedom: Schedule blocking social websites, apps, and even the Internet on all your devices.

» FocusBooster: Uses the Pomodoro Technique so you can focus on single tasks for twenty-five minutes apiece.

We live in a world where distractions are all around us. You shouldn't feel bad if you occasionally indulge in them. Instead, you should recognize that you're not perfect and proactively use the above apps to prevent distractions whenever you need to laser-focus on a task.

## #7. Create an Interruption-Free Environment

**Type:** Support habit

**Best time to complete:** Anytime

**Frequency:** Daily

**Benefit:** We've already talked about the importance of removing distractions before you sit down to the work, but there are a few additional measures you can take to remove distractions before starting a high-value task. What I recommend is to create a mini-stack that you'll complete prior to any activity that requires 100% concentration.

**Description:** First, you need to set aside thirty minutes (one time) to create a simple routine where you identify all the distractions in your life. Then you'll map out a simple process for how you'll remove each one.

Next, you will complete a five-minute habit before starting an important task. My recommendation is to have it as the last small action in a stack, which can act as a bridge between the routine and your first MIT.

Here are a few things you can add to this stack:

» Put your cellphone on airplane mode.

» Turn off your wireless router (if you're working on a deep work task that doesn't require the Internet).

» Play music or white noise that you feel helps you stay focused (see small action #9).

» Wear a pair of headphones if you work in an office (do this even if you don't listen to music, so you'll have a barrier around the people who like to interrupt you).

» Tell coworkers (and family members) that you shouldn't be disturbed during this time unless it's an emergency.

» Use any of the tools mentioned in small action #6 to block the distractions on your computer.

» Set a timer where you work at a priority task without taking a break. (My preference is the Pomodoro Technique, which I'll talk about in a bit.)

Yes, I'll admit many of these ideas are extreme. But if you're having trouble focusing on priority tasks, then you need to take an aggressive approach to controlling those interruptions that prevent you from doing great work. If you implement any of these ideas, you'll set up an environment that's completely free from distractions.

## #8. Declutter Your Desktop

**Type:** Support habit

**Best time to complete:** Morning or evening

**Frequency:** Daily

**Benefit:** It's difficult to stay focused when surrounded by chaos. Spending five minutes clearing your work area at the start (or end) of each day will help to mentally prepare you for being productive. A cluttered desk can also be highly distracting, constantly reminding you of all the *other* things you need to do. Remove these physical distractions and you'll see an improvement in your concentration.

It's not just your physical environment that needs organization. A cluttered computer not only can be distracting, but also leads to wasted time that you'll spend looking for the files you need. Get organized and you'll be instantly more productive.

**Description:** Clear all paperwork off your desk except what you will need that day. Put everything else into physical folders, file boxes, and drawers—out of sight, out of mind.

Clear your computer desktop by deleting temporary files and downloads you don't need anymore. File everything else in the appropriate folders.

## #9. Improve Focus by Playing Music

**Type:** Support habit

**Best time to complete:** Anytime

**Frequency:** Daily

**Benefit:** Science has shown that certain types of sounds and music can improve concentration or focus. Calming music, ambient nature sounds like rain or ocean waves, and simple background noise like a fan or the babble of conversation in a coffee shop may help you to concentrate and stay focused on your tasks.

If your career requires deep work where focus is crucial (like writing, finance, art, and computer programming), then you should consider playing a certain type of music during the blocks of time when you need full attention on a task.

For instance, I use the focus@will app whenever I write or simply to need to focus on an important task. This tool has a mix of up-tempo, acoustic, and ambient sounds that block out all distractions and allow me to singularly concentrate on the writing task. In fact, since I've started using this tool, my writing productivity has gone through the roof.

**Description:** Now, you don't need focus@will to improve your concentration. It costs $10 per month, which you might feel is a needless expenditure. However, I do recommend that you experiment with different types of music/sounds to see which one helps you focus the best.

I find that the best music for concentration is usually classical, ambient, or instrumental, without lyrics. You also could try a fan or air conditioner, nature sounds, or a website like Coffitivity that simulates the background noise of a busy coffee shop. There are also several white noise apps for iPhone and Android that offer a selection of different background noises.

Finally, you can find productivity playlists compiled by other users on YouTube and Spotify. Once you've found your ideal work soundtrack, play it whenever you're ready to get down to work.

### #10. Update Your Accountability PartnerType: Support habit

**Best time to complete:** Anytime

**Frequency:** Daily or weekly

**Benefit:** As we've discussed, when you're only accountable to yourself, you're likely to procrastinate on a task. That's why you should work with an accountability partner where you send a quick update about your work-related tasks.

**Description:** There are many ways to send a quick update. You could have a short Skype or phone call. You might jot down your results and send them via email, text, or instant messenger. Finally, if you don't have an accountability partner, you could use Coach.me, which combines a habit-building interface with a social aspect where members encourage one another as they hit important milestones.

### #11. Reward Yourself for Completing a Task

**Type:** Support habit

**Best time to complete:** Anytime

**Frequency:** Daily

**Benefit:** If your day is all work and no play, you'll eventually burn out. To keep your motivation high, try to add small rewards to your workday. These treats not only act as a break to replenish depleted levels of concentration, but they also work like a carrot on a stick—you'll work faster and with more enthusiasm when you have something to look forward to after completing a difficult activity.

**Description:** For each major, important task on your daily list, plan a suitable reward you'll look forward to. These treats don't have to be anything fancy as long as they feel like a treat to you—a cup of coffee, goofing off on the Internet, a five-minute yoga session, or sitting down with a magazine is just fine. The key here is to keep these rewards as small as possible, so they don't take up too much of your free time.

If you get stuck, we have a large list of rewards you can use to motivate yourself on our free companion website.

## #12. Track Time for Your Activities

**Type:** Keystone habit

**Best time to complete:** Anytime + evenings

**Frequency:** Daily

**Benefit:** Have you ever finished a workday knowing you've worked hard but don't feel like you've accomplished anything? Why does this happen? Well, this often occurs when you *overestimate* time spent on work tasks and *underestimate* time spent on disruptive activities like talking to coworkers, checking Facebook, or browsing the Internet. A quick fix to this is to track your work time.

The benefit of tracking your time is it gives you true perspective on what you're accomplishing, where you're spending the most time, and what activities are a waste of effort.

**Description:** The simplest way to track your time is to use software or an app. I recommend one of these two options:

The first is RescueTime, which tracks your time on specific programs and websites. This is the perfect solution for anyone who knows they waste time but needs more information about their "problem areas."

Rescue Time runs in the background and sends you a report at the end of each week so you'll know exactly how much time you're spending on different software applications and websites.

The second option is to manually track your time using an app. (I recommend aTimeLogger, which is a tool I use daily.) The idea here is to create "buckets" for each aspect of your job and then start/stop the timer whenever you're working on a task related to one of these categories.

I'll admit using aTimeLogger can be a bit obsessive. But it's perfect for anyone who wants to maximize their productivity by spending the optimal amount of time on the important things related to their job or business.

As an example, I currently have fifteen categories of tasks for my business. But my monthly goal is to make sure that at least 30% of my time is spent writing and 10% is spent on book marketing. Since both are an integral part of my business, I use aTimeLogger to track my tasks and verify that the bulk of my time is focused on these two categories.

As part of my daily productivity stack, I review aTimeLogger. The goal here is to make sure that I'm hitting the percentages that are important for my business. If I'm not, then I make an adjustment for the next day to make sure I do more of these two activities. (If you'd like to learn more about how I manage my time through this app, then be sure to check out the step-by-step tutorial that I've provided through the free companion website.)

In regard to habit stacking, you should track each work-related activity (if you're using an app like aTimeLogger), but you should also review the time logs at the end of the day during an evening routine. This will give you a true understanding of where you spend the most time and where you can minimize (or eliminate) certain activities.

## #13. Work in Pomodoro Blocks

**Type:** Support habit

**Best time to complete:** Anytime

**Frequency:** Daily

**Benefit:** Smart workers use time to their advantage by knowing how to ignore distractions while they're on the clock. If you're someone who has trouble focusing, then try condensing your efforts into short sprints and tracking them with a timer. A system for doing this is called the Pomodoro Technique.

The Pomodoro Technique is a popular time-blocking system created in the 1980s by Francesco Cirillo that has been embraced by entrepreneurs and work efficiency experts.

Cirillo recognized that humans can focus only for a limited amount of time before becoming distracted. He found that it's better to create a system where people focus for a condensed period and then proactively take a rest break before beginning the next sprint.

He named his technique after a popular kitchen timer that looks like a tomato (hence the name pomodoro, which is Italian for tomato). The timer was used like any old kitchen timer, but Cirillo experimented with time blocking until he discovered the most effective usage of time blocks (for efficiency in work production).

**Description:** When using the Pomodoro Technique, you:

1. Choose a task (e.g., writing).
2. Set a timer for twenty-five minutes.
3. Work for twenty-five minutes without succumbing to *any* distractions.
4. Take a five-minute break by getting up and walking around.
5. Go back to work for another twenty-five minutes.
6. After every four time blocks, take a fifteen- to thirty-minute break.

So, to put it all together, if you set aside 120 minutes for writing with the Pomorodo Technique every day, you would write for a total of 100 minutes, with three five-minute breaks between the sessions.

You might assume that this technique is not as effective as working without breaks. But think back to those times when you tried to do a task for an extended period of time. In all likelihood, you were energized at first, and then you reached a point when your concentration dropped off. Finally, you probably felt the urge to do anything *besides* your current task.

The Pomodoro Technique prevents these distractions because it keeps your mind fresh and focused. With the scheduled rest breaks, you have an opportunity to take a few minutes off to relax. So even though you're working for less time, the quality of the content will be better than what's normally created at the tail end of a marathon session.

If you're interested in the Pomodoro Technique, you might want to download one of the following programs:

» Team Viz (a program that syncs between your computer and mobile phone)

» Rapid Rabbit (iPhone and iPad apps)

» Flowkeeper (PC users)

» Pomodoro (Mac users)

» Pomodoro (Android users)

When it comes to time blocking, the amount of time you choose really depends on your personal preference. I like the Pomodoro Technique because it has a nice symmetry. The twenty-five minutes on and five minutes off adds up to thirty minutes. You can schedule these thirty-minute blocks throughout the day and use the time-tracking techniques that you just learned to make sure you're working on priority activities.

## #14. Write a "Done List"

**Type:** Support habit

**Best time to complete:** Evenings

**Frequency:** Daily

**Benefit:** Many people struggle with to-do lists because they can make you feel demotivated if you plan too many activities. So another option is to create a "done list" where you jot down all the tasks you achieved for the day. This will help create motivation about what you'll work on the next morning.

**Description:** Make a note of tasks as you complete them, or reflect at the end of the day and write down a list of everything you achieved. You can do this on paper or in an app like iDoneThis.

## #15. Identify One Task to Delegate or Outsource

**Type:** Elephant habit

**Best time to complete:** Anytime

**Frequency:** Daily

**Benefit:** Most careers have some tasks that are critical to the job and other tasks that are a waste of time. You can improve your job performance by maximizing the amount of time you spend on these high-value activities.

For instance, a salesman should increase his number of sales calls. A writer should write more. A lawyer should increase her billable hours. You get the picture.

The more time spent on these high-value tasks means an increase in your job performance and salary. So one simple way to have more time for important tasks is to identify (and delegate) any activity that gets in the way of maximizing your job efficiency.

If you have an employee, then delegate those time-consuming tasks. Or, if you're willing to spend money, you can hire somebody to take care of them. You'd be surprised at how easy it is to remove those pain-in-the-butt tasks from your life and have somebody else worry about them.

**Description:** You can outsource anything these days. My advice is to keep a running list of chores and tasks you'd like to eliminate. Create the habit where you add one item to this list daily. The simplest way to do this is to pause for a few seconds before an activity and think to yourself, "Am I the only one who can complete the task?" If the answer is no, then jot it down on your list.

Once you have a little time—perhaps after a month—open this list and use the following resources to permanently eliminate this habit from your life:

- » **Virtual Staff Finder**: Increase your productivity by hiring a dedicated and experience Filipino virtual assistant.

- » **Upwork**: Hire from a large pool of freelance web developers, writers, graphic designers, and virtual assistants.

- » **Fiverr:** Pay $5 to get tasks done—anything from graphics and design, to digital marketing, to writing and translation, to video and animation, to music and audio, and advertising.

- » **Taskrabbit**: Post an ad to hire a Tasker to help you pack your boxes, build your furniture, or run your errands.

- » **Angie's List**: Hire a fully vetted contractor to take care of that home improvement project you've been dreading.

- » **Care.com**: Sign up to search for pet, child, or senior "caregivers" and house sitters within your area.

- » **MyLaundryOnline**: An online laundry pickup and delivery service.

- » **Shoedazzle**: Take a quick style quiz and get a "personalized showroom" of high-fashion accessories and shoes to choose from.

» **Virtual Dating Assistants**: Helps you write dating profiles, send messages to matches, and set up dates.

» **Fresh Direct**: Get "groceries delivered to your door."

» **Seamless**: Order from your favorite restaurants and have them delivered to your door via your iPhone or Android.

It's amazing what can be delegated or outsourced these days. All you have to do is think of the chores and activities that get in the way of your productivity and then do a little bit of research to find someone who can take them off your plate.

## #16. Automate Your Work

**Type:** Elephant habit

**Best time to complete:** Anytime

**Frequency:** Daily

**Benefit:** If most of your work is through a computer, then you probably complete numerous small tasks that kill your productivity. Sure, each activity might only take a minute or two, but when you add them all up, the results are a significant loss of your work efficiency. Again, this is time that could be spent on high-value tasks or simply more time you could spend with your family. That's why you should consider automating certain parts of your workflow with apps like IFTTT and Zapier.

The purpose of IFTTT and Zapier is to create automated rules between two pieces of technology that you frequently use. (IFTTT calls them recipes and Zapier calls them Zaps.) One of the cooler ones I found is certain coffee makers will start brewing when your FitBit registers that you're awake. What you want to do here is automate all those small tasks that you do daily, which will free up your time to focus on the important things.

**Description:** This is an elephant task where it'll take weeks, and sometimes even months, to fully automate your life. Actually, this can be addictive because you'll start to think of all sorts of activities that can be automated.

My suggestion is to set aside a few hours to jot down all the small tasks and activities that you do every day. Be as thorough as possible because you might find a Zap or recipe that can automate these processes.

After completing this list, your small action is to pick one activity that can be automated. I'd recommend getting started with IFTTT first (since it's 100% free). But if you can't find a recipe for a regular task, then it could be found on Zapier.

## #17. Unsubscribe from an Email List(s)

**Type:** Elephant habit

**Best time to complete:** Anytime

**Frequency:** Daily

**Benefit:** Email is one of the biggest "time sucks" around. While it's now a critical part of the modern business environment, it's also a productivity killer because it means most of your day is spent sorting through junk mail and responding to pointless conversations.

Now, it's almost impossible to reach "inbox zero" as a part of your daily stack, but what you can do is unsubscribe from a few email lists each day.

**Description:** Most email management programs (like Gmail, Outlook, and Hotmail) offer a search bar in their program that help you find messages according to the keywords that you enter. You can use this search bar to your advantage by entering one simple phrase: *Unsubscribe.*

Simply fire up your email program, enter the word "unsubscribe" in the search bar, and then look at each of the messages that it brings up. Odds are, you don't really need most of the automated messages that show up. So each day, you remove yourself from these lists by opening up a few of the top messages and getting off their lists. Do this habit regularly and you'll see a dramatic decrease in the amount of daily junk email.

## #18. Research One "Side Hustle"

**Type:** Elephant habit

**Best time to complete:** Anytime

**Frequency:** Daily

**Benefit:** I'll admit that much of this career habits section is written for folks who like their jobs and want to increase their productivity. Unfortunately, there are many who hate where they work and want to do something different. If that sounds like you, then you should consider researching a side hustle as a daily habit.

A side hustle is another way to describe a part-time activity that *could* turn into a full-time income.

Now, the downside of side hustling *isn't* a lack of opportunities. In fact, the problem is there are too many choices here, which makes it hard to pick one and stick with it. That's why you need to chunk down the decision-making process where you research one side hustle every day to see if it matches your personal preferences.

**Description:** While there are countless resources you can use to research a side hustle, the best starting points are Nick Loper's Side Hustle Nation and his book *Buy Buttons*. Both provide a great overview of the different income-generating opportunities and what you need to do to create a similar business.

For this daily habit, I recommend researching a single business and asking yourself a few key questions like:

» Do I have time to work on this side hustle?

» What equipment is required to get started?

» How much money do I need to invest in it?

» Does the type of business match my personality (e.g., if you're an introvert, then a business that requires an outgoing personality isn't a good match)?

» Can this business scale into a full-time income?

There are hundreds of side-income opportunities. My suggestion is to spend time each day learning the details about one to see if it matches your preferences. You could create a simple Excel spreadsheet that's based on the above questions and then fill in an entry for each business.

If you commit this elephant habit for a few weeks, you'll start to see a pattern of the businesses that you like and the ones to avoid. Then you can make an informed decision about the business that you should pursue.

## #19. Make One Business Connection

**Type:** Keystone habit

**Best time to complete:** Anytime

**Frequency:** Daily

**Benefit:** You've probably heard the expression, "It's not what you know. It's *who* you know." Well, it's true for every area of life, but this is especially true when it comes to your career. Specifically, if you'd like a better job, then one of the best strategies you can do is to consistently build up your network by connecting with one person a day.

**Description:** There are many ways to improve your business network. My recommendation is to combine online networking websites with in-person events to build up your relationships.

Here are five resources you can use to get started:

> » LinkedIn: The best social media site for making business connections and profiling your skills, knowledge, and areas of expertise.

> » Beyond: Another social media site for professionals, with over 50 million registered members.

> » Meetup: The preferred site for finding specific groups in the area and connecting with people who are interested in your career field.

> » Facebook Groups: One of the best resources for finding people who share a mutual interest. There are millions of groups here, so it's not hard to find a few that specialize in your industry.

» Google Plus: While use of Google's social site has diminished, it's still embraced by folks in the business and technology fields. So if have a job like that, then this is a great place to look.

To get started on these websites, I recommend completely filling out your online profile. Be sure to list your skills, previous job experience, interests, and anything else that highlights your unique talents.

Next, make a commitment to contact an average of one new person every day. When introducing yourself, keep it brief and focus on making a genuine connection.

This message shouldn't be about what you'd like to "get" from this person. Instead, talk about how you share an interest in the same career and you'd like to make a connection. Include a note from something about their profile that stood out.

The same principle applies for in-person meetups. Focus on making genuine connections and how you can help the other person first.

Once you start to build up your network, look for ways to strengthen these bonds. Send them referrals, comment on their social media updates, and share anything they'd like to promote. Most importantly, post updates and links to industry-specific content to show you're someone who knows this business.

Building up your network won't pay immediate dividends. But you'll find that as you interact with new people, the occasional career opportunity will come up. And if you're someone who constantly provides value, then it'll be your name that they consider.

## #20. Review HARO for Business Promotion Opportunities

**Type:** Support habit

**Best time to complete:** Morning and evening

**Frequency:** Daily

**Benefit:** If you run a business or freelancing service, then acquiring new customers and leads needs to be an important part of your daily routine. There are many resources and strategies you can use to promote your business, but one of the best is **free publicity** that can be generated from the Help a Reporter (or HARO) website.

HARO is used by journalists to find quotes and sources for their upcoming stories. They will post a request for help with a story, and if you reach out with a quality response, you can be quoted (even promoted) in their next story—all for free!

**Description:** The trick to HARO is consistency. You won't find a request that matches your business every day. So, the best strategy is to check into the site twice a day, scan the queries in a category related to your business (e.g., Business and Finance, Education, Travel, etc.), and see if a request pops up that best relates to your business.

Once you find a query that matches your business, then schedule time into your day so you can respond back to it.

# PART VI

........................................

# FINANCE HABITS (#21 to #39)

We all know the expression "Money can't buy you happiness." But while I agree that obsessing over money is bad, I think it's important to have enough money to positively impact your life, family, and the world around you.

According to a recent survey, 38.1% of American households have credit card debt, with the median amount being around $5,700. So, true, money can't buy happiness—but I guarantee that eliminating your debt and building up a cash reserve will at least remove some major unhappiness from your life.

Improving your financial situation requires discipline and deliberate action. Really, when you think about it, the money you keep largely depends on your daily actions (i.e., your habits.) So, building a few of the following actions into your day will have a positive impact on your financial situation.

### #21. Track Your Expenses

**Type:** Keystone habit

**Best time to complete:** Evening

**Frequency:** Daily

**Benefit:** Tracking your expenses is the most important financial habit you could ever develop, but it's also the hardest because it means you must be 100% diligent and honest with yourself about your spending.

The process is simple: At the end of the day, write down everything you (and your family) purchased. Over time, you'll notice spending trends that can be curtailed. Often, this means making sacrifices and even having a hard conversation about the difference between what you "need" and what you want.

Again, it's not easy to build this habit, but it's an important one because it's the first step in the journey to mastering your money.

**Description:** Get started by keeping all the receipts, credit card statements, and notes (in an emergency) for each expenditure. Then, at the end of the day, jot down a description of the purchase and the amount. (This should be a daily habit because it's easy to forget those small purchases that you make throughout the day.)

From there, input this information into one of the following tools:

» A notebook (yes, this is a low-tech approach, but some folks like having a string of notebooks that they can use to maintain their records).

» A spreadsheet program, like Microsoft Excel.

» A Cloud-based software program and app like Mint.

There are advantages and disadvantages to each strategy, but I prefer Mint because it tracks your spending *and* provides numerous suggestions for saving money.

## #22. Review Your Financial Situation

**Type:** Support habit

**Best time to complete:** Morning

**Frequency:** Daily

**Benefit:** Let me start by repeating one of my favorite quotes by Peter Drucker: "What gets measured gets managed." When it comes to building positive finance habits, this saying is a reminder that the simplest way to control your money is to review your financial situation *daily*.

**Description:** Get started by merging all your accounts into a tool like Mint or Personal Capital. This includes your credit cards, checking account, investments, and personal assets (like your car). Don't worry: both websites use a high level of encryption to protect your sensitive financial information.

Mint is designed for people who need to stick with a budget and want to track their daily spending. Personal Capital is designed for folks who don't have a lot of debt, have a few investments, and need a single interface where they can get a full picture of their finances. My recommendation is to choose the one that matches your personal situation.

This habit is straightforward. Once a day, log into this account and do a quick scan of your finances:

» Did you make all the purchases that it records?

» Is there any spending habit that you can reduce or eliminate?

» Do you have enough of an emergency fund?

» How much credit card debt do you have?

» How much interest are you earning on your savings?

» How much are you spending (and saving) each month?

» Do you have a savings plan?

» What are your mandatory expenses?

» What are your spending triggers?

Yes, the answer to some of these questions can be tough. However, if you're willing to constantly monitor your spending, you'll be one step closer to mastering your financial situation.

## #23. Review Your Budget

**Type:** Keystone habit

**Best time to complete:** Anytime

**Frequency:** Daily and weekly

**Benefit:** Sticking to a budget is yet another tough but necessary habit. It requires that you do more than simply tracking your expenses. Here you'll think critically about your spending and look for ways to cut corners on your outgoing cash.

There are many benefits to having a budget. You'll:

» See where your money actually goes.

» Find opportunities to cut down on frivolous purchases.

» Create an organized approach to your finances.

» Understand the difference between a necessary expense and an impulse purchase.

» Teach good financial habits to your kids. (In other words, they'll understand *why* they can't have that $300 pair of distressed denim jeans.)

» Relieve stress. Even if you're not getting "good news," you'll feel in control because you're taking aggressive action to improve your financial situation.

Every household needs a budget. It's a building-block habit that will have long-term rewards as you improve your financial situation.

**Description:** There are two budgeting habits that you can build. The first is the daily checkup that fits neatly into any regular stack. Here, you'll look at your budget as a reminder of what you're allowed to spend for each category.

The second habit is the weekly budget review. This thirty-minute routine is important because it gives you a complete picture of where you're spending your money and if you're sticking to the plan.

During this weekly analysis, look at each category and ask questions like:

> » "Are my expenditures under what I've allotted for that category?"
> » "Should I increase or decrease the cap for a particular category?"
> » "Is there a type of spending that I can completely eliminate?"
> » "Why did I purchase each item? Is it because it's a need or a want?"
> » "Are there substitute habits or purchases that can minimize what I'm spending?"
> » "Can I find any additional 'financial holes' that can be plugged?"
> » "Is my money being spent on the things that truly matter to me?"
> » "What was the last item I regretted purchasing?"
> » "What's holding me back from taking action?"
> » "How would my budget look without debt payments?"
> » "What's my true hourly wage?"
> » "What can I do to increase my income?"

> » "If I died today, would my family be okay?"

> » "Am I setting a good example for my children?"

> » "Where do I want to be financially one year from now?"

> » "Do I have enough of an emergency fund?"

> » "How much am I spending (and saving) each month?"

Mastering your budget is an ongoing process. You won't get it right during the first review. Instead, use these weekly reviews to make small, incremental corrections on your spending.

Finally, you can use programs like Excel or Mint to monitor your spending, but if you want additional help, then you should check out a budgeting-specific tool like You Need a Budget. This is a multiplatform software program that's specifically designed to help you stick to a budget without feeling like you're missing out on life.

## #24. Check Your Billing Statements

**Type:** Support habit

**Best time to complete:** Anytime

**Frequency:** Monthly

**Benefit:** There are many small charges that are tacked on to your monthly bill statements, such as credit cards, cable, Internet, utilities, and ATM fees. All of them seem like a small amount, but when you add them up, the total amount wasted each month can be startling. They are the proverbial death of a thousand cuts.

By creating a monthly habit to review these bills, you can identify opportunities to reduce or eliminate your recurring expenditures.

**Description:** Once a month, go through each statement and highlight *any* questionable item. Also, if you feel that you're spending too much money in a specific category, then earmark that expenditure. You'll call this company and negotiate a lower price, which we'll talk about next.

### #25. Negotiate a Lower Price

**Type:** Elephant habit

**Best time to complete:** Anytime

**Frequency:** Weekly

**Benefit:** Another way to master your finances is to *stop bleeding money*. In other words, reducing your monthly expenditures can help you reduce your debt and/or start putting more money into your long-term investments. All of this can be achieved by calling each company and negotiating a reduction on many of those small charges.

This tactic works because most companies understand the cost of acquiring new customers. Usually, it's much lower than the price reduction you're trying to negotiate. So, if you're aggressive enough to call each account and ask for a deal (or a price reduction), you can save a bit of money on your bills each month.

**Description:** Each company requires a different approach for negotiating better terms. If you want specific scripts of what to say and how to say it, then I recommend signing up for Ramit Sethi's free email mini-course, The Save $1,000 in 1 Week Challenge.

Use the list that you compiled in habit #24, then call (at least) one company a week to negotiate better terms for your contract. Sure, this might take a month of effort (and a little bit of your soul while you listen to elevator music), but the result can lead to a significant savings on your monthly bills. This is money that can be reinvested into your credit card debt, student loans, mortgage payments, or long-term investments.

## #26. Find Coupons for Necessities

**Type:** Support habit

**Best time to complete:** Morning

**Frequency:** Daily

**Benefit:** There are some products that you are going to purchase no matter what they cost, so it makes sense to find (and use) coupons to save money on these mandatory items.

**Description:** Look through your daily newspaper or browse the Internet for coupons for necessary items like toilet paper, garbage bags, or paper towels. Cut the coupons (or print them from the Internet), then put them into your wallet so you have them next time you buy these necessities.

If you'd like to take your couponing efforts to the next level, then here are a few additional ideas you can use:

> » Learn all you can about the ins and outs of couponing. (This means setting aside thirty minutes daily to educate yourself.) Go to the sites listed below that specialize in couponing hacks:

◊ Ebates

◊ Coupons.com

◊ Groupon

◊ Amazon

◊ FatWallet

◊ RetailMeNot

◊ ShopAtHome

◊ SlickDeals

◊ Savings.com

» Get weekend subscriptions to several different local papers, which is the cheapest way to get the best deals in your area.

» Buy items because you need them, and not because they're discounted through a coupon. Purchasing unnecessary goods is nothing more than a fast-track to hoarding or even winding up in the poorhouse.

» Throw brand loyalty out the window. If your beef stew *must* be made by Dinty Moore, then couponing may not be for you. Brands should not matter. What counts is getting the necessities at an affordable price.

There are people who spend the bulk of their free time on couponing. However, if you follow the basics outlined in this section, then you can save a decent amount of money without spending too much time on this activity.

## #27. Conserve Your Utilities

**Type:** Support habit

**Best time to complete:** Morning and evening

**Frequency:** Daily

**Benefit:** Turning off the lights and appliances in your home, office, or apartment can save you a significant amount of money when it comes to your monthly utilities. Not only is it simple to do, but it also helps the environment.

**Description:** Anchor this habit to your evening and "leaving the home" routines. Here, you'll take a quick lap around your home, office, or apartment. Turn off all the lights and appliances that aren't being used, then lower the heat (if it's winter) or turn off the air conditioning (if it's summer).

To supercharge your efforts, you can add a series of tiny actions into your daily routine:

1. Turn off lights whenever you leave a room.
2. Power down electronics when they're not being used. (Many electronics will often go into "standby" mode that still uses some electricity.)
3. Open windows and use fans for cooling in the summertime, saving the air conditioning for those oppressively hot days.
4. Open the blinds and shades in the winter, which lets the sun shine in and warms your home without expending additional energy.
5. Match your pot size to the proper sized burner. Using a small pot or pan on a larger electric coil means you expend more energy to get the same result.
6. Use cold water to do loads of laundry. The results are nearly as good, but it costs about 40 cents less per load of laundry than washing clothes with hot water.

7.  Turn off the water heater if you are going to leave your home for a few days. It takes an hour to get a water heater to reheat the water and saves quite a bit of energy over the days you are gone.

I'll admit that many of these actions seem inconsequential, but if you repeat them often enough, you'll notice a dramatic reduction in your monthly utility bill.

## #28. Pack a Meal, Snack, and Coffee

**Type:** Support habit

**Best time to complete:** Morning

**Frequency:** Daily

**Benefit:** Preparing and packing the food items you consume every day is both a healthy choice and a wise financial decision. Author David Bach often talks about what he calls The Latte Factor, where a simple way to save money is to eliminate those small, recurring purchases that add up to a substantial amount of cash. You can put his advice into action by preparing your coffee (or tea) and a snack before leaving your home in the morning.

**Description:** Check your kitchen for what you could bring as a snack or for lunch. Place it with your purse or car keys so you don't forget it when you leave. Or make coffee at home and use a travel mug to take it with you.

## #29. Scan "Garage Sale" Facebook Groups

**Type:** Support habit

**Best time to complete:** Anytime + lunch

**Frequency:** Daily

**Benefit:** As I mentioned before, I have an eleven-month-old son (at the time of this writing). If you have children, then you know how quickly they go through clothing. Paying full retail price for their outfits can quickly add up to a lot of money. The good news is you can dramatically reduce this expenditure (and a whole lot more) by purchasing items from "garage sale" Facebook groups in your local area.

My wife uses these groups all the time. She frequently finds whole bags of outfits for $10 to $20. She also uses these groups to purchase discounted furniture, decorations, and a variety of consumable items.

If you'd like to build a habit that will help you save money, then you should join the garage sale groups in your area and check out the listings throughout the day.

**Description:** It's not hard to locate groups that specialize in selling and swapping items. Here's a five-step process to find groups in your area:

1.  Go to the Groups tab on Facebook or download the Facebook Groups app to your mobile phone.
2.  Enter: [Your county name or local area] + one of these words: garage sale / swap / sell / moms. (The names of these groups vary, so you need to dig a little to find the one for you.)

3. Click on the description and send requests to join the groups that cater to buying and selling used items.

4. Read the rules once you've been accepted because each group has a specific process for selling items.

5. Check in a few times a day (during a stack or when you have free time).

And if you're confused about any of these steps, then check out the brief walkthrough on the companion site.

## #30. Buy for Value

**Type:** Support habit

**Best time to complete:** Anytime

**Frequency:** Weekly

**Benefit:** Choosing quality over quantity with the things you purchase is the best way to prevent you from having buyer's remorse. This way, every time you look in your closet or at decor around your house, you won't experience the stress of not loving an item you have purchased.

In fact, one important lesson I've learned is to think of your purchases as investments. If you know you'll use an item frequently, then it makes sense to buy the best, most durable option. This can include clothes, electronics, food, furniture, and appliances. But you can also apply this logic to larger-ticket items like your home and car.

(For more on this, I recommend checking out this article on Lifehacker that talks about the importance of buying for quality.)

**Description:** This habit can take some time to master, but you should try to think carefully about the long-term consequences of each item that you're purchasing.

For example, if you are in a clothing store and you try something on and like it but don't love it, realize that you will never like it more than you do in the store. If the item does not enhance your self-esteem or your confidence, then move on to another item. But later, if you continue to think about this potential purchase, then you can always go back later and buy it.

Don't go for the cheapest option when you are out shopping. Find items that are durable and that will last, so you do not need to replace them within the next few months.

One way to find the "best" of an item is by purchasing access to the Consumer Reports website, which is widely known as the top resource for testing products and giving them rankings on a wide range of factors.

## #31. Comparison Shop for a Major Purchase

**Type:** Elephant habit

**Best time to complete:** Anytime

**Frequency:** Daily

**Benefit:** You should always research a major purchase by comparing the price on different websites. The bigger and more expensive the purchase, the more important it is to work this habit into your schedule. Not only will this save you money, it also helps you make a better-educated purchasing decision.

**Description:** Choose an item you need to buy. Explore different options on *at least* three retail websites and the magazine Consumer Reports. Check the features, details, availability, and price of the item to see which website has the best deal. Also, go through the *negative ratings* to see what people didn't like about it, and then the *positive ratings* to see what others loved about it. Look for patterns in both to get an accurate picture of what it's like to own this product.

You can take this a step further by creating a spreadsheet in which you list out the major features of your top selections. This will help you make a better-informed decision because all the data is right in front of you.

This habit isn't just for physical purchases. You can comparison shop for any high-ticket item, like vacations, insurance rates, and credit card points programs. A little bit of extra effort in research now can mean serious savings down the road.

## #32. Plan Your Meals

**Type:** Keystone habit

**Best time to complete:** Anytime

**Frequency:** Weekly

**Benefit:** We often make poor financial and health decisions due to a lack of proper planning. One reason people consume fast food is because they think about what they'll eat at the last minute and then buy whatever is immediately accessible (like something from the Golden Arches). You, on the other hand, can prevent this from happening by building a weekly habit where you plan your meals for the next seven days.

**Description:** This is a twofold habit that includes looking up ingredients and shopping for them (see the next habit). Each week, think about your family's schedule, identify the number of meals to prepare, and then map out what you'll cook during the upcoming week. Not only does this help you eat healthy, it also reduces the amount of money you spend on takeout and restaurants meals.

There are countless resources you can use to find meal plans, but my favorite is 5 Dollar Dinners, which offers a combination of meal plans, coupons, and recipes for quality dinners that won't break the bank. In fact, lately I've been slowly mastering many of the meals that Erin Chase (the owner) has featured on her website.

## #33. Prepare a Food Shopping List (and Stick to It!)

**Type:** Keystone habit

**Best time to complete:** Anytime

**Frequency:** Weekly

**Benefit:** I have to admit something: I *love* Doritos. While they are probably one of the unhealthiest foods known to man, there's something about this salty, cheesy snack that I crave. That said, you'll never find a bag of Doritos in my home. I refuse to buy them because I know that I'll succumb to my weakness one day and devour a whole bag. My strategy? Before food shopping, I write down a list and stick to only those items (which never include a delicious bag of Doritos).

I'll admit this is another habit that sounds overly simplistic. But if you build a habit of only shopping for items from a list, then you decrease the likelihood of eating junk food—and you'll save a lot of money along the way.

**Description:** Look in your refrigerator, review the meals you have planned, and check out your cupboard. Write down a list of only the items you need, and do it before you leave for the store.

Furthermore, be sure to shop on a full stomach. As you're probably aware, it's easier to succumb to a junk food temptation if your body is depleted and your mind is filled with all sorts of cravings for salts and sugars. (You can read this Cornell study to learn more about this phenomenon: Fattening Fasting: Hungry Grocery Shoppers Buy More Calories, Not More Food.)

## #34. Plan Your Daily Errands

**Type:** Support habit

**Best time to complete:** Morning

**Frequency:** Daily

**Benefit:** Planning your daily errands is like reviewing your daily budget—it keeps you on track and in control of your spending. It also helps you avoid the stores where you tend to overspend. Finally, when you map out an itinerary, you'll visit the places in the most logical order, which will save you time, gas, and money.

**Description:** Write a list of errands you need to complete. Then rewrite the list in the order you will complete each task. Make sure you stick to the list so you don't go somewhere you didn't intend to go and spend money on frivolous items.

## #35. Unsubscribe from Catalogs and Junk Mail

**Type:** Elephant habit

**Best time to complete:** Anytime

**Frequency:** Monthly

**Benefit:** Receiving a never-ending stream of print catalogs with discounts and promotions often leads to unnecessary spending. Saving 20% on a purchase isn't saving any money at all if you spend $100 to save that $20. **You didn't save $20, you spent $80.** Keep that in mind the next time you receive a catalog or coupon that's full of "savings."

If you're serious about eliminating needless spending from your life, then one of the simplest ways to do this is to get rid of junk mail and catalogs.

**Description:** I'd consider this to be an ongoing elephant habit that will require consistent effort every month if you want to get rid of all unwanted mail. You see, whenever you offer up your mailing address for coupons of "free stuff," these companies can sell your information to third-party vendors. This means that if you've signed up for dozens of offers, then you'll need to build a habit where you regularly opt out from the various places that are responsible for sending junk mail.

Get started by using a service like Catalog Choice, which eliminates *most* unwanted mailings. Usually it'll take a month or so for the various companies to follow through on your request. Then you can use the following steps to make sure you're completely off these unwanted lists:

» Go to DMACHOICE.org to get rid of unwanted magazines and newsletters.

» Go to OptOutPrescreen.com (US only) to get rid of unwanted credit card offers.

» Write to the mail preference service (for the US or the UK) to opt out your name from the major mailing list.

» Avoid placing your address on surveys, product warranty cards, and raffles.

» Ask individual senders to remove you from their mailing lists.

» Request to make your personal information confidential in the county and state database.

» Add a "No Junk Mail" or "No Free Papers" sign on your mailbox.

» Sign up to receive statements and bills electronically.

Sure, these steps require a lot of effort. But if you work at it a little bit every week or month, then you can forever eliminate the tide of worthless catalogs and mailings.

## #36. Find Something Free to Do

**Type:** Support habit

**Best time to complete:** Anytime

**Frequency:** Weekly

**Benefit:** It's possible to get out of the house and enjoy yourself without spending money, but many people often overlook this tactic because they think it doesn't sound as fun as a fancy dinner. But think of it this way: dinner and a movie for two can easily cost more than $100. This money could be better spent on groceries or paying off credit card bills.

If you take the time to research free activities in your area and substitute them for those lavish nights out, then you can enjoy something fun without it negatively impacting your financial situation.

**Description:** Dedicate five to ten minutes each week to planning your schedule. Check your local paper or community calendar, or do a quick Google search for upcoming events. Then choose a few you'd like to do and write them down in your calendar so you don't forget about them.

Here are some suggestions of fun activities that are completely free:

- » Leverage your library. Most libraries have extensive CD and DVD collections, activities for children, film nights, book clubs, and many other events.
- » Play your favorite board game with the family.
- » Figure out a walking tour. One of the truths of life is that most people only explore the history of the area they live in when people come to visit. You can be different by learning about your community and exploring it.
- » Visit a free museum or zoo.
- » Volunteer at a nearby charity or church event.
- » Set aside time to just relax and read books or watch movies.
- » Join a local club for a hobby that you love.
- » Plan a relaxing bike ride with your family in a scenic part of your area.

Notice how all these ideas are completely free? Most of the time, people gravitate to expensive activities (like a dinner out) because they don't take the time to plan ahead. But if you set aside time during a weekly stack, you can easily find fun stuff to do that doesn't cost much.

## #37. Skip the Commercials

**Type:** Support habit

**Best time to complete:** Anytime

**Frequency:** Daily

**Benefit:** You and your family are exposed to hundreds of ads daily, which can have a negative impact on your spending habits. The worst culprit is television (especially children's programming). They show a commercial, and you feel like you "need" whatever is being promoted. That's why you should attach a "commercial skipping habit" to your entertainment consumption.

**Description:** There are two ways to skip commercials. First, you can record all your favorite programs ahead of time and watch them later. Most television packages offer the digital video recording (DVR) feature, so all you have to do is program specific shows, watch them when you want, and then fast-forward through the commercials.

The second option requires a larger commitment—cut the cord from your cable subscription.

Now, I'm not telling you to stop watching TV or live like a monk. But technology is now advanced to the point where you can watch the same programming at a fraction of the cost and skip past all those annoying commercials. Let me explain:

There are streaming media devices like Roku, Kodi, or Amazon's Fire TV Stick that allow you to access most of the same programs that you normally get through a cable subscription. Each of these devices gives you access to thousands of streaming channels. Some are free and some are premium. Even if you pay for two or three 0f these services, it still results in a significant cost savings.

For instance, my setup is simple right now and only costs an average of $40 (as of March 2017), which is significantly less than the $130+ cable bill we once had:

1.  Netflix ($7 monthly)
2.  Amazon Prime ($99 per year or $8 monthly)
3.  Sling TV ($25 monthly)

With Netflix and Amazon, you can watch most of the movies, documentaries, and premium TV shows that you love. And with Sling TV, you have access to your favorite network shows. It's television-on-demand at its best, and more importantly, you don't have to sit through commercials, which are distracting and reinforce negative spending habits.

If you want to create a similar setup for your home, then I recommend checking out the book *How to Watch TV Without Cable* by Stephen Lovely. This book talks about the benefits of "cord cutting" and how you no longer need to rely on cable companies to control your viewing habits.

## #38. Set up Automatic Withdrawals

**Type:** Support habit

**Best time to complete:** Anytime

**Frequency:** Monthly

**Benefit:** You've probably heard the financial advice of paying yourself first. This means that before buying groceries, paying bills, or spending money on frivolous items, you deposit money into a long-term investment like an IRA, mutual fund, or savings account for real estate investing. The problem with this advice is that *most people don't do it.* So, a simple solution is to set up automatic withdrawals and review these transactions monthly.

I'd consider setting up automatic withdrawals to be an *anti*-habit. It's designed to remove any decision or action on your part. Instead, money comes out of your account each month without you doing a thing. This is important because it's easy to make excuses about why you need the cash for something else. The interesting thing is when money is automatically pulled from your account, you suddenly "find" ways to tighten your belt and not spend as much that month.

**Description:** The first step is to understand your financial goals and set up withdrawals to match these outcomes. Do you need to:

» Get out of debt?
» Save for retirement?
» Put away money for your children's college?
» Save for a large investment (like a real estate property)?

You should eliminate credit card debt before anything else because the interest rate is significantly higher than any interest you'd generate from any other investment. In fact, you could use the stacking method where you pay off your credit card in order from the highest to lowest interest rate.

After eliminating your credit card debt, set up an automatic withdrawal for each of the major categories where you save money (e.g., your investment account, college savings fund, and bank account). Time each withdrawal so the money is pulled out of your account right after receiving your paycheck. This is key because you don't want to see the money in your account and feel you're losing it.

Finally, review your bank statements once a month. If you've effectively implemented the other actions recommended in this section, then you might have a little bit extra left over. If that's the case, then increase the withdrawal amount for each account. On the other hand, if you're struggling to pay your bills, then you should consider lowering the withdrawal amount or looking for additional ways to tighten your belt.

## #39. Read a Personal Finance Article

**Type:** Support habit

**Best time to complete:** Anytime

**Frequency:** Daily

**Benefit:** You can never be overeducated, especially when it comes to personal finance. In fact, I recommend building a self-education habit where you read books, listen to podcasts, and scan personal finance articles. If you don't have time for these activities, then I'd recommend checking out at least one personal finance article a day.

**Description:** Here are a few personal finance websites that I'd recommend checking out:

- » Get Rich Slowly
- » Money Crashers
- » Budgets Are Sexy
- » I Will Teach You To Be Rich
- » Wise Bread
- » The Simple Dollar

If you want a simple way to scan these websites, then you can sign up for a free Feedly account, add these sites to your feed, and look through it during a regular stack.

# PART VII

## HEALTH HABITS (#40 to #60)

Your health is your most important asset. If you're not living a healthy lifestyle, then you'll severely diminish your ability to achieve goals and get the most from each day.

While you can't exercise with just a five-minute habit, there are many other small actions you can do during this limited time. In this section, I'll cover a variety of healthy habits that will support your long-term goals, like losing weight, eating better, and improving your fitness.

Let's get to it.

## #40. Weigh Yourself

**Type:** Support habit

**Best time to complete:** Morning

**Frequency:** Daily or weekly

**Benefit:** Weighing yourself regularly is a key habit for establishing clear health and fitness goals. Again: *what gets measured gets managed.* Stepping on a scale is not just for people who want to shed a few pounds. It's also a metric that can be used to make sure you stay within a target weight range.

Now, I do want to caution you: your weight will fluctuate daily, so you shouldn't be upset if you notice a few extra pounds or kilograms one day. (That's why some folks like to weigh themselves weekly.) What's more important is to see a consistency with your weight loss efforts (if that's a goal) or a steady level (if you're just trying to maintain a specific weight).

**Description:** Buy a scale and keep it in a prominent location—like your bathroom. Pick a specific time to weigh yourself and the same day of the week (if you're only doing it every seven days). Finally, write down your weight in a journal that you maintain daily. I recommend the MyFitnessPal tool for this.

## #41. Maintain a Food Journal

**Type:** Keystone habit

**Best time to complete:** Evening

**Frequency:** Daily

**Benefit:** This is a critical habit if you want to lose or maintain weight. Maintaining a food journal is an effective strategy because it makes you responsible for your actions, encourages you to avoid little "snacks," and keeps you on track to meet your health goals. In fact, one study has shown that keeping a food diary can double your diet weight loss efforts.

Food journaling is also a keystone habit because it makes you more self-aware about what you're putting into your body. Without even trying to change your diet, you'll start to avoid certain foods because you know you'll have to write them down later. This subtle change will have a positive spillover impact on your productivity, your self-esteem, and even your enjoyment of your passions.

**Description:** Again, you can use a tool (like MyFitnessPal) to get an accurate measurement of the food you're eating. Add this habit to an evening stack to make sure you're being accurate about what you eat daily. If you have trouble remembering your food intake, then do this habit twice a day—once in the morning and once in the evening. Another option is to create a habit of writing down your food intake right after each meal.

Also, be sure to log the portion sizes. In other words, don't just write "ate pasta" in your journal. Write how many serving sizes you consumed. (You can check out my article on portion control habits if you get stuck.)

Finally, be honest with your logging efforts. If you cheat, then write it down. Nobody will look at this journal besides you, so trying to hide your indulgences will only hurt you. In fact, being brutally honest with your journaling efforts might help you make a better decision the next time you're faced with a dietary dilemma.

## #42. Replace One Food Item

**Type:** Keystone habit

**Best time to complete:** Anytime

**Frequency:** Daily

**Benefit:** We all know it's important to eat healthier, but sometimes it's hard to make smart food choices when we're tired, stressed out, and overbooked. So, one simple habit you can build is to make a single food substitution each day.

Many foods have common alternatives that are a lot healthier. These choices are often lower in calories and almost always have better vitamins and nutrients. Swapping out food not only improves your health, but it can also positively impact your weight loss efforts.

**Description:** This is a simple process. In the morning, when you're planning your day, think about what you're going to eat. After going through this mental list, make a commitment to swap out just one of these items with a healthy alternative. Here are just a few examples (based on a similar cooking and prep time). You could try substituting:

- » Rice with quinoa
- » Bacon with turkey bacon
- » Soda with tea
- » White bread with whole grain bread
- » Mayonnaise with mustard or avocado
- » Ground beef with ground turkey
- » Ketchup with salsa
- » Sour cream with Greek yogurt
- » Milk with almond milk (regular milk has six times the sugar of almond milk)
- » Eggs with Egg Beaters or two egg whites for each egg
- » Vegetable oil with coconut oil
- » Croutons in salads with almonds
- » Potato chips with non- (or lightly) buttered popcorn
- » Bread with pita
- » Iceberg lettuce with arugula, romaine, spinach, and/or kale

These are just a few ideas you can use to slowly build a healthy eating habit. You'll consume just as much food, but what you eat will be of a higher quality while typically having fewer calories.

If you'd like to learn more about this topic, I'd highly recommend checking out David Zinczenko's *Eat This Not That* series of books.

## #43. Take Daily Vitamins

**Type:** Support habit

**Best time to complete:** Morning

**Frequency:** Daily

**Benefit:** Vitamins are essential because they strengthen the immune system, increase alertness, and help your body get essential nutrients.

**Description:** This habit works best in conjunction with keeping a food journal. Spend a week writing down your food intake and identifying what important nutrients you're missing. Some online nutrition tools (e.g., FitDay) will even help you determine if you are getting the recommended daily amount of each vitamin. If you aren't getting the right amounts of necessary vitamins, shop for a vitamin supplement to match your age and nutritional needs. (For more on this, check out this WebMD article on how to find the right vitamin.)

## #44. Prepare a Smoothie Drink

**Type:** Support habit

**Best time to complete:** Morning

**Frequency:** Daily

**Benefit:** If you need a quick pick-me-up, try making an antioxidant smoothie. These delicious drinks contain essential vitamins and minerals, so drinking one in the morning can give you energy that will last for many hours.

**Description:** There are a lot of smoothie recipes on the Internet, but as mentioned before, I recommend mixing up different recipes that include proteins, fruits, vegetables, potassium, and antioxidants. If you're interested in some of the ones that I typically drink, you can check out the NutriLiving website and app, which are part of the NutriBullet brand.

## #45. Fill a 32-Ounce Water Bottle

**Type:** Support habit

**Best time to complete:** Anytime

**Frequency:** Daily

**Benefit:** Even mild dehydration can cause headaches and fatigue, affect your concentration, impair short-term memory, and impede mental function. If you want to be at your most productive, it's important for your brain to be firing on all cylinders. Therefore, you should make sure you are sufficiently hydrated before starting work.

**Description:** Fill a thirty-two-ounce bottle and drink it over the next few hours. Either warm or cold water is fine—there are health benefits to both, so pick whichever you prefer. If you find plain water unpalatable, try adding ice and a squeeze of lemon.

Additionally, the rule of thumb for the right amount of water intake is eight eight-ounce glasses per day (or a total of sixty-four ounces.) This number will vary according to your weight and level of physical activity. To keep it simple, I recommend filling up your bottle twice a day and committing to drinking the entire thing. That should be enough to give you a basic level of hydration.

## #46. Wear a Step-Tracking Device

**Type:** Keystone habit

**Best time to complete:** Morning

**Frequency:** Daily

**Benefit:** Wearing a step-tracking device can have an amazing impact on your physical fitness. If you're not familiar with them, step trackers are small devices or watches that track your total steps and floors climbed every day.

At first glance, "putting on a step-tracking device" might seem like an inconsequential habit. But there are a surprising number of people who buy these devices and never wear them. If *you* start each day by clipping on this device, you'll take that crucial first step to building the exercise habit. And when you constantly wear this device, you'll find reasons to get more movement throughout the day.

**Description:** This is another super simple habit. When you wake up in the morning, put on your step-tracking device. This should be the first action you complete to start the day.

If you don't have a step tracker, then feel free to check out the exhaustive review that I posted on my website, which compares the pricing and features of the popular pedometers.

## #47. Walk between Blocks of Focused Effort

**Type:** Support habit

**Best time to complete:** All day

**Frequency:** Daily

**Benefit:** Walking is one of the best ways to get regular exercise without it negatively impacting your busy schedule. While some people (like me) prefer a scheduled time of day to get exercise, others find that it's better to walk throughout their workdays, specifically between blocks of focused effort.

If you use the Pomodoro Technique I mentioned in the Career section, then you should get up and walk for a few minutes after every twenty-five-minute block. Not only will this help you feel refreshed before the next block, it also adds a small deposit to the "bank of healthy you."

This habit doesn't neatly fit into a single stack. Instead, it should be completed throughout the day, usually after an intense block of work. My recommendation is to create a simple if-then statement, like, "Whenever I finish a work-related task, I will get up and walk for a few minutes." Sure, this might feel weird at first, but eventually you'll become comfortable with taking a walk whenever you complete a task.

**Description:** Let's do a quick bit of math, based on the assumption that you follow my advice and use the Pomodoro Technique to manage your time.

- » 25-minute blocks = two walking breaks per hour
- » Two walking breaks = eight minutes of movement (if you give yourself an extra minute to run to the bathroom or grab a drink of water between blocks)
- » Eight minutes * eight hours (a normal workday) = 64 minutes of movement

Obviously, this is a perfect-world scenario where you take a walking break twice an hour. But even if you halve that amount, that's still thirty minutes of regular exercise completed during a normal workday. That's two miles of movement on top of what you already do.

## #48. Complete a 7-Minute Workout

**Type:** Support habit

**Best time to complete:** Anytime

**Frequency:** Daily

**Benefit:** Okay, let me get two points out of the way before we talk about the benefits of this small action:

1. Yes, this is a **seven-minute** habit, so it breaks the "rules" of habit stacking. But like I said before, the five-minute rule isn't written in stone. The habits you choose can be as long as necessary to receive the full benefit of the activity.

2. No, I don't think you can get a full workout in this short amount of time. However, if you live a completely sedentary lifestyle, then completing a seven-minute daily workout is a good step in the right direction.

All that said, a great way to start or end your day is to use an app like 7 Minute Workout, which acts like a personal trainer that guides you through a twelve-exercise total-body workout. Obviously, it only takes you seven minutes to complete.

**Description:** This is another simple habit. Just fire up the app and complete the recommend exercises. (You might have to buy a few pieces of equipment ahead of time to get the real value from this app.)

Also, you should consider upgrading to their "All the Things" level, which gives you a few different program options:

- » Arms
- » Cardio
- » Core
- » Pilates
- » Toning

If you alternate between these options with each stack, you'll get a decent amount of exercise that's better than what most people do during their day.

## #49. Jump Rope

**Type:** Support habit

**Best time to complete:** Mornings

**Frequency:** Daily

**Benefit:** Starting each day with exercise gives you an immediate boost to your mood. Sure, it's not easy to break a sweat first thing in the morning, but if you do it often enough, your body will learn to crave this surge of endorphins.

Jumping rope is ideal when you don't have time to go to the gym in the morning. A quick session of jumping has many benefits. It's a full-body workout, it helps with blood circulation, it has less impact on your joints than jogging, it's inexpensive, and it can be done anywhere.

**Description:** As you wake up and listen to some of your favorite songs, grab your jump rope and start jumping on the spot. Try your best not to stop in between jumps; this is something that will come naturally if you master the exercise. Continue jumping until the song is over, and then jump into the shower to freshen up before you start the day.

### #50. Complete "Deskercise" Routine

**Type:** Support habit

**Best time to complete:** Afternoon

**Frequency:** Daily

**Benefit:** It's not healthy to sit for a prolonged period of time. This not only decreases your focus, but has also been linked to cancer, cardiovascular disease, high blood pressure, and bad cholesterol. That's why you should consider sneaking in a quick exercise routine that can be completed *without* leaving your desk. This is often cutely described as a "deskercise routine."

**Description:** The goal of a deskercise routine is to strengthen abs and legs, which are often weakened from a sedentary lifestyle. You can perform the following routine two to three times a day, while mixing in the occasional walking break (see habit #47). This is enough to give you a decent baseline level of fitness.

Here is a quick fifteen-part routine you can follow that exercises these areas:

1. Use your chair

2. Tricep dip

3. Wrists

4. Lower-body stretch

5. Spinal stretch

6. Shoulder stretch

7. Hamstring stretch

8. Side stretch

9. Buns of steel

10. Hamstring curl

11. Arm stretch

12. Shoulder blades

13. Neck muscles

14. Core strengthener

15. Ankle roll

You can do all fifteen of these movements or just a few to feel more relaxed. The key thing is to get some form of exercise throughout your workday.

## #51. Increase Your Flexibility

**Type:** Support habit

**Best time to complete:** Anytime

**Frequency:** Daily

**Benefit:** Being flexible is one of the best ways to improve your overall health. The surprising thing? While it doesn't take too long to increase your mobility, many people don't do it because they think it's too difficult.

One thing to keep in mind: according to a Harvard Medical School study, "Experts no longer recommend stretching before exercise. Newer recommendations suggest that you start your workout routine with a warm-up, such as an easy walk or a sport-specific routine such as serving some tennis balls and practicing ground strokes before a match."

There are many ways you can increase your flexibility. You could do a full-body stretch, a quick session of yoga, or a dynamic routine like Pilates. And whatever you choose doesn't have to be very long. In fact, you could easily squeeze it into a five- to ten-minute block as part of a morning stack.

**Description:** The best time to complete a flexibility routine is after your muscles have warmed up, so you should consider going for a quick walk before getting started. (Again, see habit #47). To get started, I recommend this basic stretching routine that covers seven areas:

1. Hamstring stretch
2. Butterfly groin stretch
3. Lying hip stretch
4. Lying quad stretch
5. Calf stretch
6. Shoulder stretch
7. Triceps stretch

You can do this stretching routine on an exercise mat at the end of your workout. It takes five to ten minutes. Be sure to hold each stretch for ten to fifteen seconds and repeat twice with each leg.

## #52. Practice Good Posture

**Type:** Support habit

**Best time to complete:** Anytime

**Frequency:** Daily

**Benefit:** Bad posture has been linked to long-term back pain, fatigue, and even migraine headaches. If you practice good posture, you can eliminate and prevent many of these medical issues from occurring.

Now, the difficulty with trying to improve your posture is you often must undo decades of learned behavior. These are the ingrained actions that you learned when you first started walking and crawling. You need to work on your posture daily by introducing small habits that are anchored to your existing behaviors. When you complete these actions often enough, you'll make incremental improvements in your posture.

**Description:** The simplest way to improve your posture is to create new habits for the actions that you regularly do. For instance:

» *If you're standing at the fridge to get a drink.* Double-check your feet and make sure they are correctly positioned. Take a couple of deep breaths.

» *If you're sitting down at your desk.* Check to see if you're leaning too far forward with your head and neck. (Do this whenever you sit down.)

> » *If you're standing up to pee.* Make sure your pelvis is in a neutral position and not tucked forward. Make sure that your weight is back on your heels instead of falling forward and leaning on your toes. You should be able to wiggle your toes.

> » *If you're waiting at a red light while driving.* Pull your shoulders back and square them up instead of keeping them rounded. Your ears should be directly in line with the center of your shoulders.

> » *If you're waiting in a line.* Practice your squatting position while you're staring at your phone scrolling through Facebook. (Don't worry about the people who look at you funny.)

Like the other habits discussed in this book, these actions aren't hard to complete. The trick is *remembering* to do them. That's why my recommendation is to attach one (or all) of these actions to your established routines and make them part of your day.

## #53. Meditate

**Type:** Keystone habit

**Best time to complete:** Anytime

**Frequency:** Daily

**Benefit:** Meditation helps you maintain focus on one thing (such as your breathing or the sounds of the ocean) and block out any other distractions. It has been proven to have numerous benefits, including reduced stress, improved creativity, better focus, and improved memory.

Some people meditate for hours on end, while others just take a few minutes out of their mornings. I suggest you start by meditating for five minutes so it fits neatly into your regular stack. But if you start to enjoy it, then I recommend increasing the length of your sessions.

**Description:** Find a quiet place that's free from distractions and set a timer for five minutes. Start by taking a deep breath and releasing the tension from your diaphragm. Stretch your muscles so you stay comfortable while you focus inward. Focus on clearing your mind and thinking about the present moment.

It's natural to experience frustration the first few times you meditate. If this happens to you, focus on your breathing and let your feelings of frustration dissipate. Focus on your body parts so you know when the meditation starts to take hold.

If you have trouble focusing, then try the Calm or Headspace apps, which provide specific prompts that you can use to create a relaxed state of mind.

## #54. Follow an Evening Shutdown Routine

**Type:** Keystone habit

**Best time to complete:** Evening

**Frequency:** Daily

**Benefit:** A shutdown routine is a keystone habit for getting a full night's sleep that will prepare you for a productive start to the next day.

What most folks do before bedtime is they load up on caffeine, alcohol, technology, or TV. Then they wonder why they toss and turn all night. You can break this cycle by practicing a series of habits that reduces the "noise" in your life and helps you to get into bed feeling fully relaxed and ready to sleep.

**Description:** A shutdown routine can be its own habit stack, or you can simply focus on completing a few of the following actions.

1. Don't consume any caffeine within four to six hours of bedtime. Instead, substitute it with water, a calming tea, or even cherry juice—which has been found to contain melatonin, a natural ingredient to help with your sleep cycle.

2. Avoid eating a big meal within two hours of sleeping.

3. Shut down all screened devices in the last hour before bedtime. This includes TV, phones, laptops, and tablets. You can use a Kindle device if it's just used for reading a good book.

4. Designate your bedroom as *only* for sleeping. Get rid of the TV, technology, and work-related items from this room. Do everything you can to ensure that this is only a place where you get a full night's rest.

5. Practice relaxing habits like taking a hot shower (or bath), practicing aromatherapy (habit #119), or speaking calming words like prayers (habit #110).

If you follow just a few (or all) of these practices, your head will hit the pillow feeling relaxed and prepared for a great night's sleep.

## #55. Use the Sleep Cycle App

**Type:** Keystone habit

**Best time to complete:** Evenings

**Frequency:** Morning

**Benefit:** It has been reported that the average sleep cycle is ninety minutes, which is repeated throughout the night. If your sleep patterns match these cycles, then you'll wake up feeling refreshed and energized. Using an app like Sleep Cycle will help you make sure that you're getting a full night's rest.

**Description:** Setting up the Sleep Cycle app is a simple process. First, connect your phone to a charger. Then, choose the motion detection mode. If you're using the microphone as motion detection mode, then place your phone facedown on your bedside table. But if you're using the accelerometer, then place your phone facedown on your bed. For more on this process, I recommend checking out the article published on the Sleep Cycle website.

## #56. Connect Your Location to Beeminder

**Type:** Keystone habit

**Best time to complete:** Anytime

**Frequency:** Weekly or monthly

**Benefit:** Beeminder is a habit-building app on steroids. Instead of relying on self-reporting to track your habits, Beeminder syncs with a variety of apps (like IFTTT, Gmail, FitBit, and RescueTime) to make sure you follow through with your commitments. If you fail to achieve a target goal, then Beeminder will charge you money. Sounds hardcore, right?

As you can imagine, there are many uses for Beeminder. In fact, you can use it to build many of the habits mentioned throughout this book. I recommend that you check out the site to see how it works.

In my opinion, the best use of Beeminder is to use the *location app* on your cell phone when you're at the gym and then create a "commitment contract" with Beeminder where you promise to go to this location a specific amount of time each week. If you don't follow through, you'll have to pay money to Beeminder.

**Description:** It's simple to sync Beeminder with your phone. First, set up a Beeminder account. Next, use an IFTTT recipe for your phone. Finally, turn on the notification the next time you're at the gym and create a commitment contract with Beeminder for that location. This means you'll agree to go to that location for a specific amount of time each week, otherwise you'll get fined.

Now, I don't recommend that this habit should be part of your daily stack. Instead, you should set it up one time and then review your commitment contracts every week (or month) to decide if they are worth sticking to.

## #57. Apply Sunscreen Year Round

**Type:** Support habit

**Best time to complete:** Anytime

**Frequency:** Daily

**Benefit:** While sunscreen might stay in your medical cabinet for most of the year and only come out when it's time to hit the beach or pool, UV rays can harm you year round. By applying sunscreen daily, you can reduce your chances of sunburn, photoaging, and skin cancer.

**Description:** While it may take some getting used to, the habit of applying sunscreen every day is possible to implement in your daily routine.

1. Find a high-SPF bottle of sunscreen and keep it in a place where you'll be sure to notice it, such as on your bathroom sink or dresser.

2. As you ready yourself in the morning, find a suitable time to apply sunscreen. A good time would be between showering and getting dressed.

3. Apply the sunscreen all over your body.

4. Check to see how long your sunscreen lasts. If it expires after a few hours, then bring some along with you to work or school or wherever you have to go and reapply it at a convenient time. Also, look for sunscreens that last as long as possible.

I recommend this habit whenever you'll be in the sun for longer than ten minutes. This means even if it's a cold but sunny day outside, you'll need to spend a few minutes applying a bit of protection.

## #58. Eliminate Bacteria in Your Kitchen

**Type:** Support habit

**Best time to complete:** Anytime

**Frequency:** Daily or weekly

**Benefit:** According to WebMD, your kitchen is the germiest room in your home. From the sponges to the counters to the refrigerator, there are billons of microorganisms that that could become a health hazard to you and your family. That's why you should consider a quick daily (or weekly) stack where you remove bacteria from the location where food is prepared.

**Description:** This is an easy habit that can be added to an evening stack (or become part of a weekly routine). Using a combination of disinfectants, bleach, and vinegar-based solutions, you should clean the following areas:

» Sinks

» Countertops

» Cutting boards

» Kitchen faucets

» Soap dispensers

» The dishwasher

» The refrigerator (specifically the seal and the door handles)

» Trash can

The WebMD article mentioned before provides a quick strategy on how to clean each of these areas, but I recommend one additional suggestion. After cleaning these surfaces, finish the routine by micro-waving the sponge and then leave it soaking in a bleach solution. Since this is the item that you use to clean the house, you need to take extra precautions to ensure it's 100% free from germs.

### #59. Sneeze into Your Arm, Not Your Hands

**Type:** Support habit

**Best time to complete:** Anytime

**Frequency:** Daily

**Benefit:** I'll admit this habit sounds disgusting, but it can also have a positive long-term impact on the health of you and your family. If you're sneezing into your hands, you're letting germs onto the part of your body that helps them spread the fastest. Also, there's a lack of area in your hands for particularly intense sneezes. By sneezing into your elbow, you can do your part to curb the spread of germs.

**Description:** If you've been sneezing into your hands, it might be hard to break the habit. In order to undo your reflex urge to sneeze into your hands, you need to replace this with the habit of sneezing into your elbow.

First, sneezes can come out of nowhere, which is why undoing this habit can be especially difficult. In order to prepare, just sit down and imagine you feel a sneeze coming out. Bring your elbow in proximity with your nose and mouth and make a movement similar to a sneeze.

You can even try verbalizing "achoo" or other sneeze sounds in order to help you out. Practice this for thirty seconds to one minute at a time for a few days.

Next, while some sneezes are sudden and explosive, others come through more slowly. For these sneezes, you have more time to prepare yourself. If you feel a sneeze well before it's expelled, ready your elbow in preparation.

Finally, take a moment to consider how many germs are floating around in our environment and how easily people are spreading them. By keeping germs out of your hands as much as possible through sneezing, coughing, and other actions, you are providing an invaluable service to the world.

## #60. Perform a Safety Check

**Type:** Support habit

**Best time to complete:** Anytime

**Frequency:** Weekly and monthly

**Benefit:** At the risk of sounding like a dad (which I am), there are little habits you need to build that will protect you and your family. These are called safety checks because double-checking these items might be a life-or-death action.

**Description:** This is a simple habit where you set aside a block of time each week and once a month to complete the following actions. (If you get stuck with how to do any of these actions, then refer to the owner's manual of an appliance or watch a how-to video on YouTube.):

Weekly:

- » Check the tire pressure in your car(s). Fill them if they are low.
- » Check each carbon monoxide and smoke detector to make sure they're operational.
- » Clean the lint from your dryer *and* inside the exhaust vent.
- » Check that medical alerts and contact numbers for all family members are visible on your fridge or near your phone.
- » Check all electrical sources for needed repairs.
- » Check locks on property outside the house, such as storage shed and gates to the backyard.

Monthly:

» Check your emergency flashlights to see if you need to replace the batteries.

» Check your designated place for all medical emergency equipment and make sure all are in working order.

» Check that contents of first aid or medicine kits are up to date (not expired) and properly labeled.

» Lock away all firearms and separate ammunition (as needed) from children. Use firearm safety locks.

Never underestimate the value of safety checks. Sometimes it's the small things in life that can have the biggest impact on your health and well-being.

# PART IIX

LEISURE HABITS (#61 to #74)

Engaging in leisure activities adds flavor to your daily existence. These actions can include your favorite hobbies or simply the way you choose to relax after a long day. They also include activities that directly relate to the other areas of your life. You can be passionate about your relationships, health, finances, or career.

As an example, many people view their jobs as something more than just a way to make money. For them, it's a calling that takes up a lot of their free time as they learn about their industries and network with others who share their interests.

In this section, you'll learn how to build "leisure habits." These should *always* be scheduled into your day because they create balance and help you avoid the stress that comes from trying to do too many things.

You'll find that some of these habits are organized a little differently here. Some of the entries don't strictly follow the "five-minute rule" that's recommended for most habits in a stack. But I have included them here because it's important to reward yourself with fun activities when you're focusing on self-improvement.

Let's get started with the first example.

## #61. Practice Self-Education

**Type:** Elephant habit

**Best time to complete:** Anytime

**Frequency:** Daily

**Benefit:** It's fun to learn new things on a regular basis. You could pick anything from juggling or coding to speaking a new language.

Not only do these activities challenge your mind, but they can also become an enjoyable hobby that reduces your stress. That's why you should consider practicing self-education to learn something new.

**Description:** In my book *Novice to Expert*, I talk about a lot of ways to efficiently learn new skills. Two of the strategies that I discuss are to schedule time for deliberate practice and to research what you need to learn. Odds are, five minutes isn't enough time for deliberate practice—but it's perfectly adequate for researching one skill-related topic or a challenge that you're currently facing.

As an example, one of my current goals is to complete a few triathlon races. *The problem?* I don't have a bike. So, today my "practice self-education habit" was researching the specific questions to ask when buying a road bike.

With ten minutes of research, I learned about the difference between wheels, pedals, and frame materials on a bike. While this doesn't give me an expert-level knowledge on bikes, I now know the right questions to ask when I head into the shop later this week.

Practicing self-education is a perfect task for those longer breaks during the day, like on a drive, at lunchtime, or in the evening. This is the time when you can listen to podcasts, scan through blogs, or read books that focus on one specific, interest-related challenge.

## #62. Connect with "Celebrities" in Your Industry

**Type:** Support habit

**Best time to complete:** Anytime

**Frequency:** Daily or weekly

**Benefit:** Connecting with the celebrities in your interest is a great way to increase your knowledge and enjoyment. This won't work for all hobbies (like professional sports), but if you're passionate about a smaller interest (like the game *Magic: The Gathering*), then it's not that hard to connect with the rock stars of that world. The trick is to contact them in a way that makes you stand out from the masses.

**Description:** First, it's important to remember one thing: everybody has a busy life. The top celebrities in your passion spend their time focusing on this activity, working at a job, spending time with family, and trying to relax. So, you should follow three rules before reaching out:

1.  If you are new to a hobby, stick to educating yourself through blogs, books, and forums. These should cover all the "getting started" questions that you might have. This is crucial because the last thing you want to do is waste an expert's time asking a question that could be solved with a quick Google search.

2.  Be polite in your outreach efforts. Don't expect an answer to everything you ask or get angry when someone doesn't reply. Again, we all live busy lives. So, it's not fair to "insist" a person take time out of their day to respond back to you.

3.  Begin with a simple interaction. Usually, a few sentences is enough. You can start by saying how they've inspired you, then move on to a simple question or two. Keep it short and simple because this increases the likelihood that you'll get a response. And then, if the person responds back positively, you can continue the correspondence.

It's not hard to connect with celebrities in most of the smaller industries. Usually they are the writers, bloggers, podcasters, and coaches that create great content on a continual basis. If you stick to these three rules, then you'll discover it's not hard to find and introduce yourself to these people.

## #63. Read a Book Chapter

**Type:** Elephant habit

**Best time to complete:** Anytime

**Frequency:** Daily

**Benefit:** Reading is a simple task that can provide you with benefits such as:

- » Giving your mind a workout as you learn something new or escape into a different world
- » Improving your concentration as you singularly focus on one activity
- » Reducing stress and lowering blood pressure

In my opinion, reading is a leisure habit that should be enjoyed throughout the day, but it can also provide a mental break between two difficult tasks.

**Description:** Set aside five to ten minutes to read when you feel like relaxing. A chapter is the perfect length because it is long enough to complete one strategy (nonfiction) or one scene (fiction) without it disrupting your workday.

If you're struggling to find a good book, then here are a few places to look:

» Ask for recommendations from friends, family, coworkers, and mentors.

» Google: best [genre] book.

» Google: best [genre] book [current year].

» Browse Amazon's Top 100 List (look in your preferred category).

» Join Goodreads and see what others have enjoyed in your preferred genre.

If you bring a book wherever you go, then you'll always have a way to relax for five to ten minutes during a hectic workday.

## #64. Read a Summary of the World News

**Type:** Support habit

**Best time to complete:** Morning or evening

**Frequency:** Daily

**Benefit:** We all have a responsibility to stay informed about what's going on around the world (and not just in your country). You don't need to be a geopolitical expert, but you should be able to hold a conversation about the major world events and know enough so you can make an informed decision when voting, volunteering, or donating money to charities.

**Description:** Now, I was a little hesitant to include this habit in this book because of the current political climate here in the United States. Specifically, there have been many arguments about the different news outlets and which ones citizens can trust.

My suggestion?

Instead of getting your news from *only* the outlet that confirms your world viewpoint, focus on the websites that are either "politically neutral" or that aggregate news from different resources.

Here are a couple that I like:

» Google News
» Reuters
» Associated Press
» BBC
» Newsy

You don't have to read every article, but skim the headlines and check out the items that are of interest to you. Remember that even the most well-respected news institutions are often biased in some way. It's important to form your own opinions instead of simply regurgitating what you've read online.

## #65. Learn a New Word

**Type:** Elephant habit

**Best time to complete:** Morning

**Frequency:** Daily

**Benefits:** Expanding your vocabulary comes with a wide range of benefits. You'll increase communication skills, give your brain a small workout, and improve your confidence in social situations. All of this is possible if you commit to learning one new word every day.

**Description**: There are five ways to learn new words:

1. Change your Web browser homepage to the "Word of the Day" from Dictionary.com.
2. Subscribe to a daily email, courtesy of A.Word.A.Day.
3. Buy a word-of-the-day desk calendar.
4. Download a word of the day mobile app.
5. Look up word definitions whenever you hear a new one.

Simply commit to one of these actions and focus on learning a new word to start each day. (Also be sure to learn the correct pronunciation.)

Lastly, look for a way to introduce this word into a conversation with friends, family, or coworkers. Sure, you might get the occasional odd look, but the fastest way to learn something new is to use it regularly.

## #66. Draw in a Coloring Book

**Type:** Support habit

**Best time to complete:** Afternoon or evening

**Frequency:** Daily

**Benefits:** Adult coloring books are in vogue now. Studies have shown that adults who spend just a few minutes coloring are more focused, relaxed, organized, and calm. The act of coloring can be therapeutic to anyone who regularly experiences stress in their lives.

Coloring books may be a bit of a fad, but they are backed by solid science showing the efficacy of the distraction of coloring on mental health, even for adults. Many psychologists prescribe coloring as an alternative to meditation, because it can have a relaxing and calming effect. Even Carl Jung was a fan of coloring.

Coloring has a few other benefits, such as:

» Reminding you of simpler times and temporarily returning you to younger, happier times.

» Increasing your focus and concentration. If you're having trouble with a difficult task, you can take a coloring break until you're ready to try again.

» Creating a relaxing flow state that's like other mindfulness and meditation habits.

Coloring books may not be for everyone, but if you often feel worn out and stressed at the end of the day, then taking time to do a little coloring can become a relaxing, meditative habit.

**Description:** This is a straightforward process:

1. Go to Amazon to browse adult coloring books.
2. Buy a few that look fun or match your personality.
3. Purchase markers, crayons, or colored pencils.
4. Take frequent breaks when stressed for five to ten minutes of coloring.

You might not want to carry a coloring book everywhere, like you would with a book, but if you keep one on hand at home, it can be a fun way to reward yourself between tasks or whenever you feel the need to unwind.

## #67. Do a Quick Doodle or Sketch

**Type:** Elephant

**Best time to complete:** Afternoon

**Frequency:** Daily

**Benefit:** Most children love to draw, but as adults we get too caught up in trying to make our drawings "good." We end up branding ourselves as "not creative" and never pick up a pencil again. As a result, we lose our passion for art because of a perceived lack of talent.

But doodles and sketches are not fine art. How good you are (or aren't) does not matter. Creating a quick five-minute doodle or sketch is like playtime for the brain. It's therapeutic. It helps reduce stress. It inspires creativity. It can even boost your productivity by reengaging your creative mind at a time of the day when people mostly think about what they are going to do when they get home.

**Description:** Get yourself a sketchbook and a selection of pens and pencils. In the late afternoon, when your creativity is slipping, set aside five minutes to draw whatever shapes and designs you desire. You could attempt a quick still-life sketch of objects in your kitchen, your cat, or a simple abstract doodle.

The object isn't to improve your artistic skills, so don't worry about the quality of your drawing. Just use this time to free your mind and relax.

## #68. Work on a Puzzle (or Crossword Puzzle)

**Type:** Elephant habit

**Best time to complete:** Anytime

**Frequency:** Daily

**Benefit:** Doing puzzles gives your body and mind a variety of benefits. A study done by the University of Berkeley used the brain scans of test subjects to show how puzzles can positively affect the brain and ward off diseases such as Alzheimer's. Puzzles can also help relieve stress by engaging the mind on something specific, allowing you to have an escape from your everyday life.

As an example, last year, my wife and I were limited in our choice of activities due to her pregnancy and the cold, brutal winter in New Jersey. We couldn't do the outdoor activities we usually did (e.g., skiing, snowshoeing, and hiking). So, to prevent us from "vegging out" on the couch in front a TV, we spent our nights working on a monstrous 5,000-piece puzzle.

Not only was this a relaxing way to spend time, but it also reduced some of the anxiety we both were experiencing as soon-to-be parents.

**Description:** There are two ways that you can work puzzles into your day to get the self-improvement benefits:

1.  **Solve crossword puzzles as a team:** Research has shown that working as a team can improve your speed of talking and thinking, as well as your ability to collaborate. It has also been found that puzzles can strengthen social bonds through the creation of a shared memory and group accomplishment. So, find a group of friends, family members, or coworkers, then

print off a big crossword puzzle and make it into a game. The social interaction will likely help you to burn off some steam.

2. **Grab a puzzle whenever you feel depressed:** For many people, unhappiness lies in the stressful nature of our everyday lives. Doing a quick puzzle helps to relieve this stress by deeply engaging the mind. If you feel a small bout of depression coming on throughout the day, grab a puzzle. This will help you escape in a lighthearted way.

In short, puzzles can both reduce stress and give you something to share with the important people in your life. So, if you ever need a break that doesn't involve passively sitting in front of a television, then I highly recommend building this habit.

## #69. Get Outside

**Type:** Support habit

**Best time to complete:** Afternoon

**Frequency:** Daily

**Benefit:** There is something about being stuck in a single building all day that just drains the soul. Perhaps it's the unnatural lighting or the line of cubicles. People aren't meant to be cooped inside all day long. But if you take a few minutes to get outdoors throughout the day, you'll get a regular dose of vitamin D that comes from exposure to the UV rays, which our bodies need to function.

Spending even a few minutes outside whenever you get the chance can do wonders for your physical and mental health. There is increasing evidence that shows spending more time outdoors can reduce stress, combat depression, improve sleep, and have a positive effect on your well-being. In fact, a study published in *Environmental Science & Technology* found that just five minutes of exercise in a "green" environment led to mental and physical health improvements in the study's participants.

**Description:** Every job, no matter how grueling, has breaks throughout the day. Rather than spending this time making coffee or browsing the Internet, go outside for five minutes. You can do the mindful walking that we'll discuss in habit #118, or you could look around and take deep breaths of fresh air.

Even if you live in the city, with little easy access to greenery, getting a few minutes of exposure to natural light will increase your vitamin D levels and improve your overall health.

## #70. Watch an Inspiring Video

**Type:** Support habit

**Best time to complete:** Morning or afternoon

**Frequency:** Daily

**Benefits:** Motivation is fleeting. You might feel excited one moment but then experience a crash in emotion when something negative happens. One habit that can be used to "reset" your motivation is to watch an inspiring video.

**Description:** You have a few options with watching inspirational videos.

TED Talks are inspiring lectures from the most visionary leaders of our time. They tend to be ten to twenty minutes in length, so you might need to commit to a longer habit, or watch a single video over a few days. You can access these videos directly through the TED website, but they are also accessible on a mobile app (iTunes & Android) and through a video streaming service like Roku.

If TED Talks aren't your thing, then you can also find inspirational videos on Upworthy or your favorite YouTube channel.

Watching a good video will not only give you a boost of happiness to start your day, but it can also positively impact the way you look at the world because you're constantly introducing new ideas into your subconscious.

Finally, I recommend limiting your viewing time. It's far too easy to turn a five-minute break into several hours of passively watching videos. My suggestion: stick to one video per break.

## #71. Add to Your "Bucket List"

**Type:** Elephant habit

**Best time to complete:** Anytime

**Frequency:** Daily or weekly

**Benefit:** We all have one life to live. If you're not proactively experiencing all that this world has to offer, then you are missing out. Sure, I get that you have a job, family, and infinite number of other obligations—but you should also try to expand on your long-term plans. The simplest way to do this is to create a "bucket list" of all that you'd like to accomplish in your life.

This concept was popularized in the 2007 movie called *The Bucket List*. In case you haven't seen it yet, the movie is about two men with terminal cancer who leave a hospital to accomplish all the things they've ever wanted to do before they inevitably die. Their goal is to cross off as many items from this list as possible before they "kick the bucket."

My suggestion is to create a list of your own and then regularly add to it on a weekly or even daily basis. More importantly, make a plan for how you'll check off items from this list.

**Description:** To get started, I recommend creating a list using an idea-capture device that you always have nearby. It could be a journal, a computer document, or an app like Evernote. It doesn't matter where this list goes—just make sure it's an item that's always on you.

Next, start filling out this list by answering five simple questions:

**1. "What do I want to be?"**

Imagine the different things you would like to be before you die. This can include building specific skills or roles you'd like to achieve. Simply think of the perfect version of yourself and what type of person you aspire to become.

Here are a few examples:

> » Be the best boyfriend (*then fiancé, then husband, then father*) in the world
> » Be someone my friends and family can always count on
> » Be an Ironman Triathlon finisher
> » Become a successful six-figure public speaker
> » Be a *New York Times* bestselling author

## 2. "What do I want to have?"

For some people, material possessions are important, while others don't care about the amount of "stuff" in their lives. If you're someone who is interested in enjoying the finer things in life, then you can jot down the items you want to own before you die.

Here are a few examples:

- » Have a nice home on the ocean
- » Own a vintage sports car like a classic Ford Mustang
- » Earn enough passive income to allow you to quit your job
- » Buy a nice vacation home in my favorite travel destination

## 3. "What do I want to do?"

Here, you'll determine what you want to accomplish in life. These can be small goals or a major life-defining moment.

Here are a few examples:

- » Get married to a true partner who you share adventures with
- » Have two healthy, happy children
- » Visit at least twenty different countries
- » Hike the entire Appalachian Trail

## 4. "Where do I want to go?"

It's important to visit places you've never been before. I believe you can learn a lot about yourself by traveling to a new location and having new experiences that outside your comfort zone. In this section, you'll jot down a list of the places you would like to visit.

Here are a few examples:

» Visit France and bike through the countryside

» Go to Tanzania to hike up Mt. Kilimanjaro

» Travel through all of Australia and New Zealand

» Visit all fifty states in the United States, plus Canada

**5. "What do I want to see?"**

This last question is a "catch-all" for the previous four sections of your bucket list. Here you'll write down the memories that will last a lifetime. This could be a specific event you'd like to experience or a simple moment that adds significance to your existence.

Here are a few examples:

» See the northern lights in Norway

» Watch the Running of the Bulls in Spain

» See a sunset in the Australian Outback

» Be surrounded by loving friends and family around your deathbed at the end of a long, fulfilling life

**Now, these are *my* examples. I urge you to come up with your own ideas that relate to your dreams and aspirations.** Sure, this habit might sound a little selfish and superficial, but it's important to actively think about what you'd like to do before "shuffling off this mortal coil."

Finally, I recommend adding to this list as a regular daily or weekly habit. Whenever you think of something you'd like to do, or hear of an interesting experience, take a few seconds to pop it into this list. Do this often enough and you'll come up with an extensive collection of ideas you can share with others or do on your own.

## #72. Add to Your "Soon List"

**Type:** Support habit

**Best time to complete:** Anytime

**Frequency:** Monthly

**Benefit:** In the previous habit, I talked about the concept of the bucket list. While this a habit that I personally do, I find that most people can't do much with this list because they lack the time. So, a different habit that I'd recommend is to write down the things you'd like to enjoy soon—like in the next three months.

The idea here is simple: since three months is the immediate future, you have a better understanding of what you can and can't do. And, more importantly, you can make plans to *act* on these ideas.

**Description:** Make a list of twenty fun and enjoyable things you want in the next three months. This is *not* a goals list. Instead, it's a list of fun or even odd things you can enjoy by yourself or with others. The only requirement is that each item needs to be something that makes *you* happy.

Here are a few ideas:

1. Sleep until noon on one of your off days
2. Have a movie/game night with your family
3. See a play
4. Go for a daylong hike
5. Play baseball with your son
6. Buy a new grill
7. Enjoy a date night with your spouse, away from your kids

Next, you have to make time to do these things. You'll sleep in late one day. You'll go buy that new grill. And you'll schedule time to play baseball with your son. It's too easy to fall into the trap of spending your days working, running errands, and doing household chores. But if you keep an ongoing list of fun activities, then you'll proactively create opportunities to enjoy life a little more.

## #73. Try Something New

**Type:** Support habit

**Best time to complete:** Anytime

**Frequency:** Daily

**Benefit:** Familiarity breeds contempt. We might like our routines for the comfort and predictability they give us, but over time they can become draining. If we aren't trying anything new, then what's the point of being alive?

By trying something new every day, you increase your overall satisfaction and make yourself a more well-rounded person.

**Description:** While maintaining some stability in our lives is important—such as paying bills and getting to work on time—making changes in routine and trying new things make our days exciting by giving us things to look forward to.

Here are six new things you can try:

1. **Change up your daily routine order.** If you usually shower, get dressed, and then make coffee and have breakfast in that order every morning, try switching things around. You could

make coffee and breakfast before showering and dressing instead.

2. **Try new food.** You may have become so accustomed to your favorite foods that they no longer taste all that good. When grocery shopping or going out to eat, look for items you've never eaten before and try them.

3. **Talk to someone new.** You can really gain a new perspective on life through talking to people you haven't met before. This could be someone who you work with but never interact act with, or somebody in line with you at a coffee shop.

4. **Take a different route to work or home.** You're probably so used to driving a particular way that you could practically do it in your sleep. On occasion, deviate from your usual route. This change of pace will make you feel much less like a zombie when commuting.

5. **Reduce Internet usage.** You might be used to reaching for your smartphone whenever the mood strikes, but this just lends to your complacency. Get out of your Internet comfort zone and reach for a book instead.

6. **Listen to different music.** Try music that's outside of your normal tastes. If you prefer classic rock, try rap, pop, or modern music. (There has been scientific evidence that shows this will keep your mind younger.)

Changing up your routine doesn't require a large daily time commitment. Really, all you do is switch up one routine or action. Sure, you won't enjoy every experience, but this habit will also keep your mind from going stale from doing the same thing over and over.

## #74. Enjoy a Distraction

**Type:** Keystone habit

**Best time to complete:** Anytime

**Frequency:** Daily

**Benefit:** Throughout this book, I've emphasized the importance of avoiding distractions to focus on what's truly important in your life. But if your daily existence becomes a constant list of goals, habits, projects, and chores, then you'll quickly burn out. That's why it's important to enjoy the occasional distraction between blocks of effort, at the end of the day, or even during a "mini-vacation" where you spend time doing an activity that you love.

**Description:** Whenever you feel stressed or simply want to unwind after a long day, treat yourself to a reward like:

- » Drinking a glass of wine or a beer
- » Playing a video game
- » Watching your favorite TV show or movie
- » Indulging in a sweet or chocolate
- » Dining out at a fancy restaurant
- » Getting a manicure and pedicure
- » Knitting or crocheting
- » Checking out social media
- » Socializing with friends and family

There are countless ways to reward yourself—and, sure, some of them will take longer than five minutes. That's why you should only do them after you've completed the critical daily tasks. But it's important to proactively plan fun activities just as you would with any other habit. That way, you're not just singularly focused on working, exercising, or getting things done.

# PART IX

ORGANIZING HABITS
## (#75 to #90)

Never underestimate the benefits of being organized. To be honest, growing up, I was a bit of a slob. But I've now discovered that organizing and structuring my environment in a mindful way has helped every aspect of my life. (Plus, it's nice to know where I can find my shoes before a run.)

You don't need to go overboard with organization. All that's required is five to ten minutes per day to create an environment that's free from clutter. In this section, we cover a variety of small habits that will help you bring more organization into your life without making you feel overwhelmed.

## #75. Fix Your Broken Windows

**Type:** Support habit

**Best time to complete:** Anytime

**Frequency:** Daily

**Benefit:** To be clear, I'm not talking about the windows in your home. Instead, it's the broken windows theory mentioned in Part IV that discussed how making small cosmetic changes to your surroundings will create an atmosphere that prevents a feeling of stress or overwhelm.

Examples of "broken windows" include:

> » Unmade beds
> » Piles of unsorted laundry
> » Dishes in the sink
> » Messy kitchen
> » Piles of mail, bills, and random paperwork

» Children's toys, clothing, and similar items

» Full trash and recycling bins

Sure, you might think these small messes aren't a big deal—but surrounding yourself with piles of clutter will often create a stressed, overwhelmed feeling about your life. If you take a few minutes in the morning and evening to fix your "broken windows," then you'll create a positive mindset that will carry over into other areas.

**Description:** Your choice on when to fix these broken windows depends on your personal preference. If you'd like to start the day feeling organized, then make it part of a morning stack. But if you don't like to end the day with "open loops," then complete this habit as part of an end-of-the-day stack.

Once you've picked a time, create a small routine where you take care of the messes that cause you the most stress. For example, if you come down in the morning and see a pile of dishes in the sink and paperwork on a table, spend a few minutes cleaning/organizing these items before starting your workday.

## #76. Make Your Bed

**Type:** Keystone habit

**Best time to complete:** Morning

**Frequency:** Daily

**Benefit:** I hate writing about habits that seem obvious, like brushing your teeth, eating your vegetables, or making your bed. But in life, sometimes the smallest of actions can have a powerful impact on your daily success.

In a commencement speech at the University of Texas, US Navy Admiral William H. McCraven said the following to the graduating class:

> If you want to change the world, start off by making your bed. If you make your bed every morning, you will have accomplished the first task of the day. It will give you a small sense of pride, and it will encourage you to do another task, and another, and another. And by the end of the day that one task completed will have turned into many tasks completed.

So, yes, making your bed might seem like a "little" thing, but completing this habit daily can provide many positive benefits:

» Creating a positive mood where every subsequent time you enter the room your mood will lighten as you see this fresh and clean area.

» Decreasing your levels of stress because you've reduced one less "thing" to worry about.

» Creating a sense of accomplishment. Productivity is simply stringing together accomplishments. By making your bed, you quickly check off the first task on your list and build momentum for the rest of the day.

» Reducing any type of embarrassment when someone visits your home and the room looks messy.

Yes, making your bed seems like a major habit, but just remember the advice from Admiral McCraven: "If you want to change the world, start off by making your bed."

**Description:** I won't tell you "how to make your bed" because I'm sure this is a skill that we've all learned at some point in our lives.

But if you get stuck, I recommend watching this video, courtesy of Howcast.

## #77. Clean One Refrigerator Shelf

**Type:** Elephant habit

**Best time to complete:** Anytime

**Frequency:** Weekly

**Benefit:** If you have a large family (or simply live with others), then your refrigerator is chock full of leftovers, perished food, and old condiments. And if it hasn't been cleaned recently, there are probably a variety of dips and spills that are caked on to a diamond-like hardness.

Put simply, refrigerators can become a disgusting mess if they aren't cleaned on a regular basis.

That's why I recommend a revolving "one shelf a week" cleaning habit for your fridge. This frequency means you will basically clean your entire fridge once a month, but you'll do it piecemeal, where you're constantly sorting items and getting rid of items that nobody is interested in eating or drinking.

**Description:** Once a week, identify a section of your refrigerator to organize. Get started by emptying that section. Look at the expiration dates and condition of these items, then throw out anything that's questionable. If you feel an item is about to expire, then make a mental note to eat or prepare it for an upcoming meal.

Next, clean this area of the refrigerator with an all-purpose spray and dry the shelf.

Finally, place the items you decide to keep back on the shelf in an organized order.

## #78. Leave Shoes at the Door

**Type:** Support habit

**Best time to complete:** Anytime

**Frequency:** Daily

**Benefit:** Taking off your shoes before entering a home is a custom in countries like Japan, which shows respect for the home and its owners. But it's also a great habit to build because it stops the spread of germs that your shoes pick up, and it prevents you from tracking in elements like rain, snow, dirt, or mud.

**Description:** When you come home, take off your shoes and put them in a designated spot, such as a corner or on a mat. Encourage guests and others in your household to do the same. There is a chance that you'll be asked why this is necessary. You can respond with some easily understandable reasons, such as:

» Our shoes make immediate contact with the ground, and germs are sure to exist there. By walking through our house or someone else's with shoes on, we're exposing ourselves to far more germs and bacteria than we might realize.

» Shoes are bound to get dirty. Even if you're just walking up to your front door, you can catch some dirt. By taking off your shoes as soon as you enter, you can help prevent further uncleanliness from spreading in your house.

» By having a designated area for shoes in your front entrance, you can reduce stress in tracking them down. This is especially beneficial for those with young children who are prone to misplacing things.

This simple habit can do wonders for your efforts to keep your home clean and organized. And the best part? It takes only a few seconds to do whenever you walk through your door.

### #79. Identify a "Home Base" for Every Possession

**Type:** Elephant habit

**Best time to complete:** Anytime

**Frequency:** Daily to weekly

**Benefit:** "A place for everything and everything in its place." This quote best describes the goal of any organization system—to have a specific location for *every* item in your home. This is important because knowing where all items belong removes the guesswork when cleaning and organizing items in your home.

**Description:** Here is a small list of ideas for where to place the common items in your home:

» Car and house keys on a hook next to your front door

» Purses, backpacks, and briefcases in a section near the front of your home

» Shoes in your garage, "mud room," or a location where it doesn't matter that you track in water, dirt, or grass

» Personal items (e.g., wallets, watches, and wearable devices) on a nightstand

» Cell phones and tablets "docked" in charging stations

» Children's toys in bins, shelves, and buckets

- » Detergents, fabric softeners, and other dangerous chemicals in an elevated spot away from children

- » Mops, brooms, and other cleaning items on designated hooks

- » Tools (e.g., hammers, wrenches, screwdrivers, drills, and tape measure) in a toolbox or shed

- » Out-of-season items in your attic or basement

Sure, I'll admit some of these locations might seem like common sense, but a surprising number of people store their items in a haphazard manner and then wonder why they can't find anything. By designating a "home base" for each item, you'll make it much easier to clean and organize your home.

## #80. Put Away Three Items

**Type:** Elephant habit

**Best time to complete:** Anytime

**Frequency:** Daily (one to four times)

**Benefit:** Clutter doesn't happen all at once. It's built slowly over time because people don't take an extra minute to put away their possessions. But when you commit to putting away three or more items every few hours, you'll minimize the level of mess in your life.

**Description:** First, make sure that every item in your home has a designated spot (as described in the previous habit). In other words, don't do what most people do by throwing items into a "junk drawer." That's not cleaning. That's taking random items and putting them somewhere else.

The next step is to create a habit based on if-then statements. Your goal here is to think of new set of rules where you carry items with you whenever entering a new room.

For instance, my wife and I have a rule in our house: whenever one of us needs to carry an item up or down the stairs, we leave it by the landing. Then, when one of us walks up the stairs, we grab this item and put it away in its "home base." Our logic is that since we're already making the trip, we might as well bring something with us.

Finally, you should practice this habit throughout the day. If you commit to putting items away as you move through your home, you'll never fall into the trap of being surrounded by piles of mess and assorted clutter.

## #81. Eliminate One Item

**Type:** Elephant habit

**Best time to complete:** Anytime

**Frequency:** Daily

**Benefit:** We just talked about putting away items throughout the day. But perhaps instead of putting away an item, you should just get rid of it.

There are a few benefits of eliminating "stuff" from your life:

» You can make money by selling items in Facebook groups (see habit #29), on Craigslist, or at a garage sale that you run every year.

» You can receive a tax deduction that you'll report at the end of the year.

» You are helping another person get a free or heavily discounted item that they need.

» You get to clear up space in your home by removing clutter that is no longer needed.

» You will become more selective about the items you choose to purchase in the future.

Bottom line: if you regularly get rid of your clutter, you can reduce stress and receive a few financial benefits along the way.

**Description:** First, you should create a three-box system for items that you'd like to eliminate. Label them as Sell, Donate, and Toss.

Next, while cleaning and organizing your home, look for items that you no longer need, like old clothes that don't fit, or the bread maker gift that you never used, or toys that your children have outgrown.

You can make quick decisions here by asking yourself two questions: "When was the last I used this item?" and "Why am I still keeping it?"

If it's been over a year since you've used this item and you can't come up with a valid reason for why you're holding on to it, then get rid of it.

## #82. Clean Your Office Desk

**Type:** Elephant habit

**Best time to complete:** Afternoon

**Frequency:** Daily

**Benefit:** Many people spend a significant amount of time at their desks, so it makes sense to create an organized system to allow you to quickly find any item. Unfortunately, this can be hard to do if you're constantly pulling out files, taking notes, and leaving items all over your desk.

That's why I recommend a simple habit: at the end of each day, take five minutes to organize your desk. This way, when you arrive in the morning, you're not surrounded by piles of junk and assorted clutter.

**Description:** This is a straightforward seven-step process:

1. Remove at least one nonessential item from your desk (repeat daily until you've completely decluttered your workspace).

2. Put away supplies in your desk drawer.

3. Keep cords organized using twist ties or even bread tags.

4. Throw away any trash. (Make sure that a trash can is within reach.)

5. Go through your physical inbox, scan what can be scanned, and store them digitally.

6. Set aside five minutes and clean your desk before you officially end work. (Keep cleaning materials within reach.)

7. Finish by wiping down your desk.

This is perfect for anyone who struggles with distraction or overwhelm while working. If you do it regularly, you will start each day with a clean space that allows you to focus on the day's most important tasks.

## #83. File Away Loose Paperwork

**Type:** Elephant habit

**Best time to complete:** Anytime

**Frequency:** Daily or weekly

**Benefit:** It's easy to find yourself surrounded by piles of disorganized paperwork, like bills, magazines, junk mail, and important documents. This creates a problem because when you need to find something, you'll waste time sorting through this mess. If you want to improve your organizational habits, then you need to commit to the practice of filing paperwork daily or during a single block of time at the end of the week.

**Description:** First, you should create a basic filing system that you use to organize your paperwork. (Here's a link to 18 items that I recommend for your home office.)

Next, you should create the following folders that are broken down into a few key categories:

**Legal records**

- » Birth certificate
- » Social Security cards
- » Passports
- » Property deeds
- » Car titles
- » Wills

## Financial records

» Loan records

» Lease records

» Banking records

» Credit card statements

» Investment records

» Tax returns

» Income and expense records

## Insurance records

» Medical records

» Auto, life, and home insurance policies

## Miscellaneous records

» Major purchase/repair documents

» Warranties

» Owner's manuals

» Education records

» Employment records

The golden rule for paperwork (or at least when it comes to the government) is to hold on to your paperwork for seven years. Whether you follow this advice or not, you should at least put files from a previous year into a box that's put into storage for at least a few years.

Finally, after setting up this folder system, you should follow this five-step process whenever sorting paperwork:

1. Put bills (and other items that require a response) into a pile that you'll process each week.

2. File all important items into their designated folders.

3. Create a pile of advertisements or coupons that interest you. Put them in a folder that you review once or twice a month.

4. Shred or rip up any advertisements, credit card offers, and other pieces of junk mail, or keep them in a pile that will remind you to remove yourself from their mailing list (see habit #17).

5. Read cards and personal letters. Put in a place where you can respond and hold on to them.

It's not hard to prevent those piles of paperwork. The trick is to organize them on a daily or weekly basis. Simply follow the five-step process that I just outlined to forever eliminate this one challenge.

## #84. Scan your Paperwork

**Type:** Elephant habit

**Best time to complete:** Anytime

**Frequency:** Daily or weekly

**Benefit:** There is nothing "wrong" with storing paperwork in a filing cabinet like I just described. However, if you only keep hard copies, then you risk losing them forever if you ever have a fire or flood in your home. If you're someone who deals with a lot of important documents, then you should consider scanning and storing them in a digital Cloud-based service.

**Description:** First, I recommend picking one of the three high-speed scanners that I recommend here. I like these options because they simplify the scanning process by processing multiple sheets of paper instead of the one-page-at-a-time system like you get with cheaper scanners. Plus, each document is fully searchable, which means you can use keywords or tags to quickly find a specific item.

Next, after digitizing these documents, you should store them in a Cloud-based service like Dropbox, Box, or Google Drive. This gives you full access to all your important paperwork, regardless of where you are in the world.

Third, if you have a huge amount of paper clutter, or you are creating a digital filing system from scratch, then this will be a long project that could take an entire day. But you can also create an elephant habit where you commit to scanning paperwork for five to ten minutes a day. That way the task won't seem dull and monotonous if you're breaking it down into small chunks.

Here's the process that I recommend for scanning these documents:

> » Be sure to *always* keep physical copies of important documents like tax returns, marriage certificates, birth certificates, social security information, investment files, and wills.

> » Use your speed scanners to create a digital copy of your paperwork. Depending on the type of scanner you use and number of documents you're working with, this process can take anywhere from a few days to a month. Just keep at it until all of your paperwork has been digitized.

» Use a standard naming convention so you can easily find these files. You could add a description of the item with the date it was received. Example: Costco_Receipt_2_7_17.

You don't have to be surrounded by file cabinets full of paperwork. Instead, you can digitize and store the documents that you receive daily. Not only will this declutter your life, but it also creates an organizational system where you can quickly locate any important document.

## #85. Use a Standard File Naming Convention

**Type:** Support habit

**Best time to complete:** Anytime

**Frequency:** Daily

**Benefit:** One of my pet peeves is receiving a file from someone without a clearly defined name, like an image titled IMG07663. I store many files on my computer, so I often use the search function to find an item (if I can't immediately find it in the folder where it should be located).

The reason I get peevish about a bad file name is when I save it to my computer, I know it might get lost in my folders—unless I take that extra step to use a good naming convention. That's why I recommend building the habit of creating a standardized process for naming your files.

**Description:** Here is a simple three-step process to follow whenever you're adding a file to your computer:

1. Identify the specific project this file is attached to (e.g., work, hobbies, or taxes).

2. Describe the purpose of this document (e.g., mortgage statement, blog post, book chapter, or marathon training plan).

3. Include the version number if you're working on something that has many drafts (e.g., (rough, second, or final draft).

To give you an idea of how this looks, as I type these words, the version of this section is titled Habit_Stacking_Part_9_First_Draft.

As you can imagine, the folder where I store these files is full of lots of items, but with a few seconds of searching, I can immediately locate this item. (Plus, if I ever accidentally save it to the wrong folder, I can quickly locate it by running a search on my computer.)

You don't need to use my naming convention, but I do recommend having a consistent format for your files that will simplify the process for locating and identifying all of your important digital documents.

## #86. Declutter Your Smart Phone

**Type:** Elephant habit

**Best time to complete:** Anytime

**Frequency:** Weekly or monthly

**Benefit:** Even though phone storage capacity is constantly increasing, many people often run out of space. If you want to keep your smartphone responsive and avoid the dreaded "Storage Almost Full" error message, then you should consider getting rid of the electronic clutter that you've built up over the years.

**Description:** Depending on the frequency with which you add items to your phone, I recommend doing the following either every week or month. Here is a simple five-step process to keep your smartphone up-to-date and free from clutter.

1. **Close down open apps.** Some people don't realize that when you open a new app, the old app stays open in the background. This increases the amount of energy your device uses, which is one reason why your battery might be constantly drained. I suggest you make it a daily or weekly habit to close all your open apps.

2. **Delete the apps you don't use.** If you can't remember why (or when) you downloaded an app, then get rid of it. Odds are you won't miss it.

3. **Get rid of your content, including photos, videos, and documents.** You can store these items in Cloud-based services like Dropbox. Only keep the items that you refer to constantly (like your favorite videos or pictures of your children).

4. **Delete old podcast episodes or audiobooks.** If you're like me, then you listen to a lot of audio content. Unfortunately, these files take up a large amount of space and aren't automatically deleted when you've finished them. You occasionally need to go into your preferred podcast and audiobook apps to get rid of old files.

5. **Organize your music files.** Music files can be another big space killer on a phone. Rather than downloading music files to your phone, you should consider taking advantage of streaming services like Pandora, Spotify, and Apple Music.

Nowadays, almost everyone uses a cell phone. Unfortunately, since it's a digital device and there is no visible sign of clutter, it's easy to store too many apps, photos, and files. This slows down the processing speed and maxes out your storage.

The problem here is that when you don't have enough space on your phone, you'll feel the "need" to upgrade to the next model. So you end up paying for another gadget that increases your debt. But you can fight this problem by completing the five-step habit that I just detailed every week or month to delete unused items from your phone.

## #87. Maintain a Cloud-Based To-Do List

**Type:** Support habit

**Best time to complete:** Anytime

**Frequency:** Daily

**Benefit:** One of the biggest ways to become disorganized is to keep your to-do lists on random scraps of paper or Post-it notes. A simple fix for this is to keep a list in a Cloud-based service, which allows you to easily add items, review your daily tasks, and check off errands that you've completed.

Not only will this help your personal productivity, but it also allows you to access this list if you're on different devices (like your phone, tablet, or computer), which is a great way to keep your life organized.

**Description:** This is a simple task. Simply download one of these apps and use it for all of your daily tasks and chores:

» Todoist (this is my favorite)

» Omni Focus

» Nozbe

» Remember the Milk

» Wunderlist

Once you've installed one of these apps, add all your tasks and projects to it. (In the free companion website, I provide a quick tutorial on how I use the Todoist app for all my tasks.)

## #88. Store Your Great Ideas

**Type:** Keystone habit

**Best time to complete:** Anytime

**Frequency:** Daily

**Benefit:** We all have brilliant ideas from time to time. Unfortunately, we'll often jot them down on the nearest item, like a scrap of paper. This is a dangerous practice for two reasons: 1. It's easy to lose single pieces of paper. 2. You don't have a regular system to review these ideas.

My suggestion is to choose a single device where you capture all of your thoughts, musings, and ideas. That way, whenever inspiration strikes, you can write it down in a device that you *know* will be reviewed later.

**Description:** This is a habit of process. In other words, you should train yourself (by using if-then statements) that whenever an idea occurs to immediately jot it down in your idea-capture device.

Now, there is a challenge here: we live in a modern world that's full of amazing options for taking notes and storing ideas. I would argue that these multiple options are a drawback because when you need to find a specific note, you'll need to go through all the programs that you regularly use. That's why I recommend a simple tool like Evernote that allows you to store all your content in one place that can be accessed anywhere in the world.

Besides that, there are a few other options like:

- » Moleskine Journal
- » Microsoft One Note
- » Google Docs
- » Nozbe

We've all had the occasional "million-dollar idea." Unfortunately, it's easy to fail to take action because you don't have a system for storing and processing these thoughts. If you create a habit where you put all your ideas into a central location, then you'll have an ongoing archive of all your great thoughts.

## #89. Plan a Morning "Getting out the Door" Routine

**Type:** Support habit

**Best time to complete:** Evening

**Frequency:** Daily

**Benefit:** There are few things worse (from a psychological standpoint) than starting the day feeling rushed and disorganized. If you're running around in the morning like a headless chicken, then these feelings will create unnecessary stress that can negatively impact your workday.

Fortunately, there's a simple solution. In the evening, compile all the items you'll need for the next day and put them into a central location. Then, when you wake up in the morning, every item you need will be in this predesignated spot waiting for you to leave.

**Description:** This is another habit that's simple to build. In the hour before going to bed, think of the items that you'll need for the next day and then spend five minutes putting them together.

These can include:

- » Paperwork
- » Briefcase or backpack
- » Schoolbooks
- » Laptop or tablet
- » Personal items like your wallet, keys, purse, or cell phone
- » Lunch, snacks, water bottle, and travel mug
- » Gym clothes
- » Items for your children (toys, clothes, formula or stored breast milk)

Start by reviewing your calendar for the next day, then think about what you'll need for each activity and appointment, and finally put these items in the same location where you put other items, like your wallet, purse, and car keys.

If you can commit to building this evening habit, then you'll eliminate the stress that many feel in the morning as they get ready for work.

## #90. Say "No"

**Type:** Elephant habit

**Best time to complete:** Anytime

**Frequency:** Daily

**Benefit:** Saying "no" is something many people—me included—struggle with. Sometimes it's hard to turn down someone because you want to be a nice, helpful person. On the other hand, if you're committed to many important goals, then sometimes it's necessary to decline any offer that doesn't align with your desired outcomes. These are the times when you need to say no.

Derek Sivers puts it perfectly: "If you're not saying 'HELL YEAH!' about something, say 'no.'"

**Description:** This is another "as needed" type of habit where you'll do it only when faced with a pitch or offer that doesn't match what you'd like to do in life. I recommend a four-step process for declining offers in a tactful manner.

First off, you must embrace the idea that it's okay to say no to people. I have found most folks are sympathetic when it comes to being turned down. And, in my opinion, anyone who gets mad at you for not being interested in an offer is someone you don't want in your life to begin with.

Second, you need to examine the opportunity cost of every offer. I've learned the hard way that saying yes to one thing means you say no to something else. That means if you agree to an additional task or project, then this will eat into the time you can dedicate to your family, goals, health, and work projects. Plus, it can cause additional stress and anxiety.

Third, you should create a list of criteria of what types of opportunities you'll accept (or won't accept). For instance, in the past few months, I've created a rule that I'll only be interested in projects that will help me write and promote my books. Anything that doesn't fit this requirement gets an automatic no.

Finally, saying no to somebody doesn't mean you have to be rude about it. I recommend a few simple rules for managing your correspondence with people:

> **Create a buffer.** If you're someone who receives a lot of pitches and offers, then you should consider creating a "contact you" page that clearly lists what types of offers you'll accept and what you're not interested in seeing. (Here's an example of the one that I use.)

> **Give a reason why.** You are not making excuses here—you're providing a value reason why you're unable to respond to an offer. Usually a statement like this works well: "I am working on the __ project right now and simply don't have time to work with you on ___."

> **Make your decision quickly.** Don't waste time analyzing each opportunity. Like the quote from before, if something isn't an automatic "hell yeah," then your default decision is to say no.

> **Encourage a follow up (optional).** If you feel a project isn't right for you now, but you might be interesting in the future, then encourage the person to follow up down the road. What I like to do is give a specific date range of when I might be

interested. Then I'll leave it up to the other person to contact me again.

Saying no is a crucial habit to develop. When you do this enough, you can open the door wider for those projects and opportunities that can truly add value to your life and the important people in it.

# PART X

RELATIONSHIP HABITS
(#91 to #108)

Relationships give significance to our lives. In a perfect world, you should spend as much time as possible with friends and loved ones. Unfortunately, most people treat their relationships with casual negligence because they're often the first thing to be cast aside when "life gets hectic."

The truth is, relationships require nurturing.

If you work at them daily, you'll form a lasting bond with friends, family, and other important people. That's why I recommend incorporating some (or all) of the small actions mentioned in this section.

## #91. Do an Activity That Makes You Happy

**Type:** Keystone habit

**Best time to complete:** Anytime

**Frequency:** Multiple times daily

**Benefit:** It's hard to be happy with your relationships unless you're first happy with yourself. Before you can worry about being the pleasant, likeable, and fun person that others love, you may need time to work on your mindset.

While taking a few minutes of "me" time is always important, this can be critical whenever you feel surrounded by negativity. A few minutes of relaxing time can change your perspective and make you more pleasant for others to be around.

**Description:** This is one of the few habits I recommend including in multiple stacks. In the morning, you can clear your mind to get ready for the workday. In the afternoon, do something during your lunch break to recharge your batteries. And in the evening, add an energizing habit that gets you out of "work mode" and helps you relax.

There are a lot of habits you can do in five minutes or less. Here are a few ideas to help you get started:

- » Write in a journal
- » Have a cup of tea/coffee and think about nothing at all
- » Sit outside and feel the sunshine on your face
- » Cuddle/play with a pet
- » Read a few jokes and laugh a little
- » Listen to a favorite song
- » Dedicate five minutes to meditation
- » Stop and smell the flowers—literally
- » Eat a bite of chocolate
- » Take a short walk, even if it's just around the hallways
- » Get a quick massage
- » Dance around the room like no one is watching
- » Enjoy a piece of fresh fruit
- » Read a few pages of fiction

Sure, some of these ideas might seem silly, but that's the point. When you take the time to unwind and not focus on your to-do list, you'll discover it's easy to add happiness to your life and relieve a little bit of stress.

## #92. Introduce Yourself to Someone New

**Type:** Support habit

**Best time to complete:** Anytime

**Frequency:** Daily

**Benefit:** Have you ever headed out the door to run a few errands, take a walk, or just grab some groceries and silently wished, "I hope I don't see someone I know," because you don't want to end up in a lengthy discussion?

We all do this because having conversations all the time can be tough. You have to push through awkward silences, discover topics of mutual interest, and find something to say when you ask a question and the only response is a yes or no. Sometimes having a conversation with a casual acquaintance can be emotionally and even physically exhausting.

So why do I advocate introducing yourself to a complete stranger every day?

There are a few reasons:

» You will improve your conversation skills because you'll learn the art of small talk.

» You build your confidence as you discover initiating conversations isn't hard.

» You will learn about new experiences that can be found by meeting someone who has a different view of the world.

» You can build a network of acquaintances.

» And you might even meet a potential love interest.

Now, I'll admit that not every conversation will be great. Sometimes it will be awkward, and occasionally you'll deal with people who want to avoid talking and would rather spend time on their phones. But even if 99% of the attempts go nowhere, the remaining 1% means you'll meet almost four great people per year who will have a significant impact on your life. That's a big deal if you ask me.

**Description:** It's not hard to find new people to meet. Get started by thinking about your daily routine and when you're surrounded by new faces. This could include visiting a coffee shop, the bookstore, your neighborhood park, the gym, or even when you're standing in line. These are all perfect opportunities to strike up a conversation and introduce yourself.

There are also a few basic "rules" to consider when striking up a conversation:

First, the talk should never last more than five minutes. Anything longer than that means you'll probably wear out your welcome. Just interact for a little bit, and then end it. In other words, don't be the person who won't shut up while the other person is looking for a way to escape.

Next, the simplest way to start the conversation is to be natural. The discussion should be a mix of what's going on in your immediate environment or an interesting item that you noticed about the person. In other words, don't stress over *what to say*. Just use any environmental cue to start talking.

From there, look at the person's body language for cues to keep going. If he or she gives a one-word response and is staring intently at the phone, then that's a sign that this person is not interested in talking. And if the person shows a lack of interest in talking, then it's okay to stop talking. Just remember: we all have those moments when we're not interested in having a conversation.

Now, if a person positively responds back, then you should follow up with a few questions like: *What do they do for a living? Why are they at the place you are at? What is their favorite hobby?* This shouldn't be an inquisition. Instead, you're trying to get to know the person better.

Just remember the important aspects of body language that'll make you more likeable:

» Smile

» Make eye contact

» Keep a relaxed body posture

» Hang your arms by your sides (instead of crossing your arms)

» Offer a handshake (at the end of the conversation)

» Be slow and deliberate with your responses

Meeting new people and having conversations doesn't need to be hard. Like any skill, if you work at it daily, it will become increasingly easier with time.

Just remember: if you want make new friends or find that special someone, then the best way to do this is to step out of your comfort zone and open yourself up to new potential friendships.

For more on this skill, I highly recommend Patrick King's "Conversation Tactics" series, which covers the different scenarios you'll encounter when meeting and talking to people.

## #93. Contact One Person on a Dating Site

**Type:** Support habit

**Best time to complete:** Anytime

**Frequency:** Daily

**Benefit:** Dating sites can overwhelm us with options. It can be difficult to keep focused when you see so many viable candidates for dating. By keeping yourself disciplined and contacting only one person a day, you'll be able to lessen the feeling of frustration associated with asking out a huge number of people in a short burst.

**Description:** I'll admit the following advice might sound old-fashioned—especially in the age of instant-gratification websites like Tinder, where the standard dating strategy is to swipe-left/swipe-right until you find a match.

But look at it this way: since you're competing against dozens or even hundreds of people in your area, it makes sense to take an extra step to stand out from the masses.

That's why I recommend this five-step strategy to get the best results from contacting one person daily.

1. **Make a list of traits you don't want from a partner**, such as smoking or excessive drinking. Rule out any profiles you come across with those undesirable qualities. Remember, you're looking for the perfect match for *you*, so be ruthless with your criteria. It doesn't make sense to date someone who doesn't fit your core values.

2. **Match their values.** If someone talks about the importance of their Catholic faith, and you're an atheist, then you shouldn't

bother messaging this person. This is the inverse of the previous item. Never expect someone else to change what's important to them in order to date you.

3. **Make sure you aren't messaging someone purely based on looks.** While physical attraction is important in a relationship, you also need to have personal compatibility. Look at what they write in their profile to see how it would match your lifestyle.

4. **Keep your initial message short, funny, and interesting.** Something like "How's it going?" is likely to be passed over. Look for something notable on their profile and ask about it. Or write something pithy but witty. In other words, don't give the person a tome to read as a first message. Usually, a paragraph or two is more than sufficient.

5. **Make a note of people you want to contact later.** If there are a bunch of people to message, that's great. Make sure to limit it to one person a day, but remind yourself of those who you can contact the next day, and so on.

You'll be surprised at the effectiveness of this daily habit. Whereas most people (usually guys) take the lazy route and contact dozens of people with the same message, you can stand out by sending a personalized, compelling introduction.

I won't lie to you and say this works all the time, but if you do it often enough, then your messages will stand out from the dreck that's usually found with online dating.

## #94. Give a Compliment

**Type:** Keystone habit

**Best time to complete:** Anytime

**Frequency:** Daily

**Benefit:** Giving genuine compliments is a great way to make others feel good while improving your self-esteem. Compliments have many other benefits like:

» Encouraging those who are struggling

» Strengthening existing relationships

» Serving as an icebreaker when meeting someone new

» Helping you see the good in others

Overall, complimenting people daily is a keystone habit because it forces you to constantly look for positive attributes in everyone you encounter. And if you're naturally shy or withdrawn, giving compliments forces you to interact with others, which increases your confidence.

**Description:** Keep an eye out for something you genuinely like or enjoy, such as someone's outfit, something they said, or a recent accomplishment. Then compliment the other person about it, doing it in front of other people (if possible).

Let's take a more detailed look at "how" we should compliment people to get the most out of our compliments (both for them and for us):

1. Never compliment someone "just because." Fake flattery just makes you a suck-up, and it's easy to notice someone who

gives out false praise because they think it will win them friends.

2. Compliments should always be derived from taking notice of something genuinely praiseworthy. One important aspect of this habit is you should give people 100% of your attention, instead of being distracted by your phone or something else you're doing.

3. What you say should be specific. While "you look great today" may sound good, it's better to point out a change, like a new haircut or a piece of clothing.

4. Never use a backhanded compliment. I have heard "you are a good runner for an old guy" more than once. Compliments like this sting more than they encourage.

5. Share your compliment with others, not just the person you are complimenting. Follow the age-old adage "praise in public; criticize in private."

6. Say what you mean and mean what you say. As long as your thoughts are not dirty or hurtful of others, share your compliments with others. People often fail to compliment because they assume someone already knows the compliment for a fact. Or they think that they must be constantly complimented. Even if this is true and someone has heard a compliment 500 times before, it still feels good to hear it for the 501st time.

Never underestimate the power of compliments when it comes to your friends, family, and romantic partners. As I mentioned in the introduction, it's the little things in life that solidify and enrich our relationships. If you make it a point to point out something complimentary to the people you interact with daily, it will do wonders for how you're viewed by others.

## #95. Hug One Person

**Type:** Support habit

**Best time to complete:** Anytime

**Frequency:** Daily

**Benefit:** There is something magical about a hug, isn't there? By embracing someone or something, you can make yourself feel so much better. It isn't in our imaginations, either. A variety of studies have shown the benefits of hugging, from reducing stress to helping lower blood pressure to plain making us feel good.

**Description:** Hugging requires the consent of two people, so you don't want to ambush people with hugs if they aren't expecting it. However, there are plenty of acceptable ways to hug one person a day.

» **Hug a loved one every day.** If you live with a spouse or significant other, then hug them on a regular basis. It could be in the morning, or when you both come home. By hugging them regularly, you are reminding them how much they mean to you.

» **Be social.** Going out regularly is great for hugging, as you are likely to come across people you know, and they'll appreciate a warm embrace. If you are introduced to somebody new, don't be afraid to give them a hug as well.

» **Surprise people.** If you have an elderly relative in a nursing home, they will be thrilled by you dropping by to visit them.

This is a great opportunity for you to give them a hug that they will cherish.

» **Practice hugging.** There might be days where there's no one around to hug. If this happens, find something like a pillow or stuffed animal and embrace it with all your might. The best part about hugging inanimate objects is that you don't have to worry about hugging it too hard.

Hugging is a simple way to express your positive feelings for another person. If you make a habit of doing it with the important people in your life, then you'll create those positive emotions that make the day seem a little brighter.

## #96. Text an Encouraging Message

**Type:** Elephant habit

**Best time to complete:** Anytime

**Frequency:** Daily

**Benefit:** Sending an encouraging daily text is about more than encouraging the people in your life. It's an action that also makes you feel better about yourself.

You don't need to text anything earth shattering or important. A text message is not the place for the important things that need to be said. Instead, it should be a few kind words that will make the other person feel good.

**Description:** Set aside two minutes every day to send a heartfelt text message. Focus on someone who could use a bit of encouragement, like a spouse, child, sibling, parent, friend, or coworker.

The person you text could be facing an upcoming challenge, which could be an important project, a big athletic event, a test, or a tough personal challenge. Simply write a short message wishing them luck and let them know that you're thinking of them.

You could also send a message to someone who you have not connected with in a while. Text this person a quick message saying that you have been thinking about them lately and hope they are doing well.

Making this a part of your daily routine helps you create a quick, easy, and convenient way to get a positive message to those in your circle of relationships. This may make them feel a little bit better and will certainly give *your* mood a positive boost.

## #97. Leave a Caring Note

**Type:** Support habit

**Best time to complete:** Morning

**Frequency:** Daily

**Benefit:** As I discussed in the introduction, leaving a note for a friend, family member, or loved one is a little action that goes a long way. It can brighten someone's day and show the other person that you went out of your way to make him or her smile. It's easily the best small action that does a great deal to strengthen relationships.

**Description:** The process is simple. Write a quick, uplifting message on a Post-it note or piece of paper. It's similar to the habit of texting an uplifting message to someone. The goal is to say a brief message, like "Have a great day," "I love you," or "Good luck with the project/

test/presentation." Really, the only important element is to show the other person that you're thinking about them.

Where you post this message depends on the relationship. You could leave a note on a pillow, in your child's lunch, on a desk, or in a backpack or briefcase.

Finally, you shouldn't overthink these notes. Keep them simple, speak from the heart, and say something encouraging to those you care about.

## #98. Return Calls and Text Messages within 24 Hours

**Type:** Support habit

**Best time to complete:** Anytime

**Frequency:** Daily

**Benefit:** Communication is a two-way street that leads to a healthy relationship. When someone has reached out to you, it's important to reciprocate and continue the conversation by replying as soon as possible. Returning calls and text messages in a timely manner builds trust in any relationship.

This habit seems simple. You might say, "Returning a phone call or message—there's nothing to it." However, this isn't easy for the people who live busy, overbooked lives. In fact, as a bit of an introvert, I often dread making calls to people I don't know well. It is incredibly easy to procrastinate on this task and plan to call back "later." Sometimes "later" ends up being seven days after receiving the message.

So, if you're someone who constantly forgets to follow up with people, then you should consider building the habit of returning all phone calls within twenty-four hours.

**Description:** Check for missed calls first. Return calls in the order they were received. Apologize for missing the call and inquire about what you can do for the other person. Then respond to any text messages that have gone unanswered—again in the order received. Finally, check any emails that are sitting unopened in your inbox and respond accordingly.

One tactic that I use is to schedule a daily block of thirty to sixty minutes of "flex time" into my day. This gives me time to return lengthy phone calls or text messages that require an immediate response. And when I don't have any calls or texts to return on a particular day, I use this flex time to reward myself with a treat (see habit #11).

## #99. Check Your Social Schedule

**Type:** Support habit

**Best time to complete:** Anytime

**Frequency:** Weekly

**Benefit:** One of the tackiest things you can do is to cancel your plans with other people at the last minute. Or even worse, not show up at all. Sure, there are those occasional emergencies that are out of your control, but if you always cancel at the last minute, then I guarantee that your friends and family don't appreciate your inconsiderate behavior.

A quick fix to this is to review your schedule on a weekly basis to catch any potential conflicts. This includes looking for double-booked appointments, *too much* time scheduled for a specific event, *too little* time scheduled for an event, or any appointment that risk running longer than expected.

When making social plans, it's important to allot the right amount of time for each event. This makes it easy to have a healthy social life that's balanced with all of your other obligations.

**Description:** First, all of your activities should go into the same calendar. This means sitting down and looking at all the sources where you may have written down information on any social events.

These can include personal notebooks, email, Post-it notes, wall calendars, and your mobile device calendars.

It makes no sense to have your schedule in a few different places. Instead, it should be consolidated into a single system that can be accessed at all times, which is why I recommend using Google Calendar or a similar app.

Next, add regular social events like dinner dates, lunches, events with friends (like a ballgame), meeting for coffee, and a "date night" with your spouse or significant other. These should be scheduled into your life because they help maintain relationships, while also providing balance to your day-to-day routine.

Third, be sure to block out time for routine activities like doctor's visits, gym time, grocery shopping, haircuts, and various activities for your children. These should go into your calendar to avoid mix-ups or any potential double bookings.

Finally, if you find that you have two events or appointments booked at the same time, reach out and ask if there is another day or time you can meet. Don't forget to apologize for your scheduling mistake.

There is little you can do when your boss unexpectedly makes you work four extra hours. But keeping your events organized means the fault will never rest on your shoulders and gives you the best chance to have a bit of a social life, even with a busy schedule.

## #100. Share Something Inspiring

**Type:** Support habit

**Best time to complete:** Anytime

**Frequency:** Daily

**Benefit:** Sharing quotes, stories, and articles online can bring a small bit of joy to your friends and family. If you're like me, your social media timeline is filled with constant negativity. Instead of being someone who shares the doom and gloom of the world, you can add positivity to the world by sharing fun stuff on social media.

**Description:** Now, I don't believe it's "essential" to post updates on Facebook, Instagram, or Twitter numerous times throughout the day. Let's face it: we have more important things to deal with than updating our social accounts. In my opinion, it's better to live a real life, not a virtual one, right? That said, if you make it a habit to share something positive every day, then you can help others a little by making them laugh or smile.

This is a simple habit. Spend up to five minutes daily on Google, Twitter, and Facebook to look for good quotes, articles, or blog posts. If something puts a smile on your face, then be sure to share it with others.

Finally, if you can't find anything positive during your normal social media time, then it's okay to just stop for the day.

### #101. Learn a New Joke

**Type:** Support habit

**Best time to complete:** Anytime

**Frequency:** Daily

**Benefit:** Humor is the ultimate icebreaker. If you're meeting people for the first time or you need to break the tension in a conversation, then a good joke can be helpful. Here are a few reasons why learning a new joke can be beneficial.

Humor:

> » Can make someone laugh and ease tension when meeting them for the first time
> » Is a great conversation starter
> » Builds trust and likeability
> » Breaks tension and relieves anxiety in social settings
> » Helps you think creatively
> » Is linked to living a healthier lifestyle

Injecting a bit of humor into your routine is a great way to improve your life, so let's talk about how to build the habit of learning new jokes.

**Description:** First, a word of warning. While humor can be a useful conversation tactic, *you need to know your audience*. In other words, certain types of humor are only right for certain situations. The dirty jokes that get you a ton of laughs while hanging out with your buddies watching football probably won't work in a corporate or social environment. Therefore, I focus on learning clean (or mostly clean) jokes.

The process of learning a joke a day is simple. Use Google search to find a joke that makes you laugh. If the joke makes you laugh, it will likely tickle the funny bone of a few others. Read it over a few times to help you memorize it, and/or write it down to review later.

Don't try to force your jokes into a conversation. Wait for down times or the right minute to tell your joke. You may not even use the joke every day. But the time you spend memorizing a single joke every day will give you a nice repertoire of humor to draw from when the moment is right to inject a bit of humor.

Being able to make someone else laugh is a great conversation starter. Having a joke to share is always a great thing because getting someone to laugh is usually the first step to growing or strengthening a relationship.

## #102. Research a Fun Activity

**Type:** Support habit

**Best time to complete:** Anytime

**Frequency:** Weekly

**Benefit:** We've already talked about how planning a fun activity can be a great way to save money, but it's also a habit you can do to enrich your relationships. The problem that some people have is they tend to do the same thing again and again, until they get into a rut. Subsequently, your relationships will stagnate because your activities become boring and predictable. The solution is to set aside time each week to come up with a few interesting events you can share with people in your life.

**Description:** I recommend using a mix of nine resources to find fun events in your area.

**1. Eventful.com**—Eventful is a great website for anyone who lives in or near a big city. It does a wonderful job of aggregating sports, festivals, concert tour dates, performing arts, nightlife, conferences, wine tastings, family events, and comedy shows.

**2. Local Newspapers, Magazines, and Websites**—Narrow down your search to your local area, which can be found in region- or town-specific newspapers, magazines, and websites.

Also, any mid-sized or larger town will have a local "alternative" paper, which often has an events & activities section. Here, you'll find listings that feature everything from concerts and bar band appearances to local bake sales and community dance classes.

**3. Google**—You may have an idea of something cool to try and just not know how to get started. This is where a little Googling can be a powerful strategy. Simply go to Google.com and type in the name of your city or town, plus one of the following terms:

- » Event listings
- » Festivals

» Cooking lessons

» Softball leagues

» Running clubs

» Volunteer opportunities

» Concert venues

» Mini-golf

You can try to input any search parameters for these. The larger the town, the more opportunities there will be to find unique and interesting events. But even smaller towns have fun activities that are only known to residents.

**4. Map out a Walking Tour**—Many people live in an area but never visit the cool places 100 miles around where they live that are places tourists want to visit. You could take your "research fun activity" time and try to set up a nice walking tour of some semi-local areas, as if you were a tourist rather than a local.

**5. Only In Your State**—The website Only In Your State has a massive collection of articles that feature interesting, state-specific attractions. It's similar to BuzzFeed, where each list has a specific clickbait-style headline. But I love this site because it has a lot of great ideas for interesting activities to check out in your local area.

For example, while writing this section, I did a quick search for New Jersey and found a bunch of fun-sounding events, attractions, and towns to check out, including:

» 12 Reason Why the Jersey Shore Isn't Just a Summer Destination

» The Hidden Park That Will Make You Feel Like You've Discovered New Jersey's Best Kept Secret

» The 14 Towns You Need To Visit In New Jersey In 2017

» 8 Unforgettable Road Trips to Take in New Jersey Before You Die

» The Easy 1-Mile Winter Hike in New Jersey That's Positively Bewitching

I'll be the first to admit these headlines sound hokey, but if you check out this website, I guarantee you'll find an abundance of fun activities to share with the people in your life.

**6. Try Geocaching**—In *The Shawshank Redemption* (one of my favorite movies), the protagonist, Andy Dufresne, tells his friend Red to go on a scavenger hunt for a hidden item when he gets out of prison. He gives him the basic coordinates and then says, "In the base of that wall, you'll find a rock that has no earthly business in a Maine hayfield."

This movie quote encapsulates the spirit of Geocaching. You are given GPS coordinates, then it's your job to find the hidden clue that will reveal a hidden stash. With this strategy, you can turn a simple walk into a fun experience that you share with friends and family.

**7. Bulletin Board Flyers**—Some events may be too small to even get much notice in the local paper. But if you keep an eye out for bulletin board flyers, you'll discover a number of smaller local events that are worth checking out.

**8. Craigslist**—The website Craigslist is a useful resource to find listings for fun activities, interest-specific groups, volunteering opportunities, local events, and classes. How useful these listings are varies greatly on your local Craigslist site, but it's worth checking out once or twice a month.

**9. Meetup.com**—The website Meetup.com is a great place to find groups based off your personal interests and make new friends as you enjoy one of your favorite activities. Simply do a search within two to fifty miles of your home, and you will find lots of groups you can join. But like Craigslist, the quality (and size) of the groups depend on how many people in your community use the site. If you live in a small, isolated area, then you might have to drive far to connect with a group that matches your personal interests.

These nine tools for finding fun activities are just a sampling of ways you can find activities in your area and connect with new people. There are literally thousands of apps, websites, and newspapers designed to help you find fun activities. But this plethora of options can make you feel overwhelmed, so my advice is to pick a few resources from this list and then spend five to ten minutes each week finding interesting activities to explore.

## #103. Know What Your Significant Other Likes

**Type:** Support habit

**Best time to complete:** Anytime

**Frequency:** Daily or weekly

**Benefit:** Understanding the wants, desires, and goals of your spouse or significant other is an essential part of maintaining a healthy relationship. As I've mentioned numerous times, relationships are often built on small things. If you focus on becoming a person who constantly thinks of your partner, then you'll be on the road to building a relationship that stands the test of time.

**Description:** Get into the habit of taking notes on what your significant other enjoys. As an example, you may be out shopping and notice that your husband expresses interest in a specific Dewalt Miter Saw. Or maybe your wife is talking about a specific scarf she likes. Take note of this, and then buy this item as a gift for the holidays or their birthday, or simply as a surprise present.

This habit shouldn't be limited to "big purchase" tickets. It can also be used effectively for small things. For instance, if you remember that your wife said that she would love to see a certain movie, then you can schedule a surprise date night to go see it with her.

The notes on your significant other can be kept anywhere, but I feel the best tool for this is Evernote. You should create a Notebook for your significant other (and for the other important people in your life, like your parents, children, siblings, and close friends). Then you'll build a habit of regularly adding interesting ideas and events like:

» Movies they want to see

» Favorite TV shows

» Restaurants they casually mention they'd like to try

» Events or activities they might enjoy

» Items they express an interest in purchasing

» Dates, like their birthday, your anniversary, and upcoming important events

The key to this habit is to jot down this information as soon as possible so you don't forget about it. As soon as you think of something, pull out Evernote and then pop it into the app.

Surprising that special someone in your life with an unexpected gift will do wonders to strengthen your relationship, but more importantly, it lets them know that you listen and remember the small things they often talk about.

## #104. Pause Before Discussing Sensitive Topics

**Type:** Support habit

**Best time to complete:** Anytime

**Frequency:** Daily

**Benefit:** There is a great quote about conflicts and arguments: "10% of conflicts are due to difference of opinion and 90% are due to wrong tone of voice."

I'm sure these percentages are *not* scientifically accurate, but there is a lot of truth to the underlying message—conflicts most often arise from *how* you say something rather than *what* you say.

That's why it's important to build a habit where you pause (for at least a few seconds) before engaging in a sensitive conversation. This will give you enough time to consider what you want to say and how you want to say it. Done correctly, this habit will minimize the arguments that often arise when there is a difference of opinion.

**Description:** The way you share your viewpoints sets the stage for how other people will react. By pausing and thinking of a diplomatic way to say the exact same thing you originally intended, you also set the stage for a peaceful conflict resolution.

Here's how this works:

1. Identify those "crucial conversations" that require careful, measured responses.

2. If conversation has started, listen carefully to what the other person is saying.

3. During these discussions, pause for a moment to give yourself time to think of what you'll say next.

4. Take a deep breath.

5. If the other person has valid points, try to acknowledge these points in your response.

6. Respond in a carefully measured tone, instead of rushing your response.

7. Maintain this slow pace throughout the conversation, resisting the temptation to let your emotions get the best of you.

Following these seven steps will do wonders for decreasing the number of conversations that lead to conflict or even outright hostility. All of this can be possible if you build a habit of taking short pauses to control your emotions before responding to a potentially sensitive subject.

## #105. Outline Your Thoughts before a Difficult Conversation

**Type:** Support habit

**Best time to complete:** Anytime

**Frequency:** Weekly

**Benefit:** In potentially high-stress situations, emotions can run rampant. This can include difficult conversations like:

- » Asking a boss for a promotion or pay raise
- » Firing an employee
- » Talking with a friend or family member after an argument
- » Confronting a spouse about a specific behavior or action
- » Admitting a mistake that you have made

These conversations can be intimidating or even terrifying, but if you outline your thoughts beforehand, then you'll know what you want to say and how to best phrase it.

**Description:** By outlining your thoughts in advance, you give yourself time to fully develop your thoughts in a healthy manner, rather than jumping the gun and making decisions based on emotion.

Here's a simple process to think about what you'll say:

First, write down your thoughts and feelings. Start by observing what emotions you are feeling (e.g., fear, anger, anxiety), and then write down what thoughts or experiences are causing these feelings.

Next, ask yourself if you know these thoughts are true. For instance, if you're worried about a meeting with your boss because you think you'll be fired, ask yourself if you know for certain that this is a real possibility and what evidence you have that supports this thought. Most of the time the fears that we build up in our heads are nothing more than fears.

Third, think about a past intimidating situation you dealt with. *What did you do right? What did you do wrong? What will you do this time?* Understanding how you dealt with a similar conversation can be the key to figuring out the best approach with this upcoming discussion.

At this point, you'll be ready for any conversation. By going through this exercise, you'll get the fears out of your head and down on paper. This will also give you a chance to mentally rehearse what you'll say based on the responses of the other person. The more you go over this conversation in your mind, the better equipped you'll become to handle any difficult discussion.

## #106. Pause to Control Your Anger

**Type:** Support habit

**Best time to complete:** Anytime

**Frequency:** Daily or weekly

**Benefits:** There are times when we're not in control of our anger, but instead our anger controls us. Regaining control of our emotions on these occasions is essential because these are the moments that often lead to poor choices that can have a severe negative effect on your life.

When giving in to anger, you make bad decisions, communicate poorly, say hurtful things, lose track of logic, and blow things out of proportion. Even when you have a good reason to be angry, losing your temper means you'll end up doing something you'll regret later.

The simplest fix to this problem is to pause for a few seconds (even up to a minute) to gain control of your emotions, and then think carefully about how you'll respond.

**Description:** Whenever you feel anger, the first thing to do is immediately remove yourself from the situation. This means walking away from the person (you can make an excuse that you have to use the restroom.)

If that's not possible, then walk to another part of the room, direct your attention toward something else (like looking out a window), and give yourself a moment to gather your thoughts.

Next, use imagery to relax a little. Visualize a relaxing moment from your memory or imagination—something you would really enjoy, like sitting on a beach sipping a fruity drink.

Be sure to breathe deeply, from your diaphragm. Shallow breathing from your chest won't relax you, so picture your breath coming up from your "gut." Take a long, slow breath—the inhalation should last a second. Hold your breath for another second and then take a third second for a long, slow exhale.

When you inhale, think of clean, pure thoughts and happiness filling your body. As you exhale, imagine all the anger, tension, and stress going out of your body. Slowly repeat a calming word or phrase, such as "relax" or "take it easy." Keep repeating it to yourself while breathing deeply.

When you take these simple ten deep breaths, your problem will not disappear—but you should have changed your perspective enough that you can deal with the conversation in a logical and rational manner where you're not overly swayed by emotion.

Finally, it's perfectly normal to be angry occasionally. But if it seems like you're constantly pissed off, then you might have an anger issue. This is the point where you should seek professional help and get feedback on how to control your emotions.

## #107. Practice Active Listening

**Type:** Support habit

**Best time to complete:** Anytime

**Frequency:** Daily

**Benefit:** It is easy talk to people *without* giving them our full attention. Often, these discussions happen while we're engaging in activities like working, playing a game, checking Facebook, or watching television at the same time. Not only is this disrespectful to the other person, but it also means you can't fully comprehend what they have said.

If you want to improve your relationships, the simplest strategy is to fully engage in each conversation, without doing any of the distracting activities that I just mentioned. In other words, whenever you're talking to someone, you're not looking at your phone, TV screen, or other people. Instead, you're talking back and forth, responding to every nuance of the discussion.

Not only does this habit show that you're paying attention, but it's simply the polite thing to do when a person is talking to you.

**Description:** There are five steps you can use to actively listen to others:

1. Stop what you are doing. You cannot actively listen if there are other distractions. Give the person in this conversation 100% of your attention and focus.

2. Make eye contact. This is the *key* part of body language communication because it shows the other person that you are interested and paying attention to their words.

3. Just listen. Don't interrupt, give your opinions, or attempt to fix their problems. Simply listen to what they are telling you.

4. Wait for a natural pause to ask clarifying questions. Use this if you don't understand what is being said. You can also use pauses to repeat back major points, such as, "I hear you saying _____."

5. Be empathetic. Try to feel what the speaker is feeling. If the story is sad, try to feel sad with them. If it is something they are angry about, share in their anger.

These are just a few steps you can use to become a better listener. The key point here is that whenever someone is talking to you, it's only fair to give them your undivided attention. In our modern world, people live distracted lives where they're always *sort of* paying attention. If you act differently than the masses, you will become known as that special someone who fully engages in all your conversations.

## #108. Photograph Important People (and Events)

**Type:** Support habit

**Best time to complete:** Anytime

**Frequency:** Daily

**Benefit:** Pictures help connect us to both those who came before us and those who will come after. They help tell the story of family members and ancestors who took part in shaping how the world is now. According to educational psychology, self-identity plays a big role in self-confidence. This means that documenting your life and the people in it can help to boost your well-being. And the simplest way to do this is to build a habit where you photograph the people, places, and possessions that matter to you.

**Description:** While it's easy to get distracted—especially during important events—and not get your camera to capture the moment, make a point of documenting your life on a regular basis. That way, you'll have a timeline of each year showing its highlights and special moments.

To document your life, I recommend these tips:

» **Buy a high-quality camera:** This may be an expensive camera where you can adjust the aperture, shutter speed, and ISO picture setting. Or you can use the camera on a high-quality smartphone.

» **Carry your camera with you:** While it may just seem like a typical night out with friends, make sure you have your camera with you so you can capture these special moments. You never know—what seems like an everyday occurrence right now might become a prized memory in the future.

» **Don't wait until everyone is camera ready:** Sometimes the best moments are captured when people aren't expecting a photo. Take candid pictures of people enjoying themselves so you can have an authentic memory of the people who are important to you following an event.

» **Back up your photos:** Make sure to use a reputable backup service to store your pictures, such as Dropbox or Microsoft OneDrive. Also, consider buying a portable hard drive that can give you an extra level of backup.

In the words of the immortal Ferris Bueller, "Life moves pretty fast. If you don't stop and look around once in a while, you could miss it."

There's nothing you can do to prevent time from marching on, but if you continuously document your life with photographs, you'll have a digital archive of all that you've experienced and the people you share it with.

# PART XI

## SPIRITUALITY HABITS
## (#109 to #127)

Let me start this section with a simple question: "What is spirituality?"

The answer will be different for different people.

Many feel spirituality represents a deep connection with the god of their choice. Others prefer to follow an "enlightened life" of wisdom and compassion. There are some that feel spirituality is simply having quiet "me time" to reflect on the things that matter to them. And finally, there are folks who find a spiritual connection through helping others.

I firmly believe there is no right or wrong type of spirituality. The only thing that's important is to focus on habits that are important to you. These are the beliefs that fill you with "a peaceful, easy feeling" (as the Eagles once sang).

Consequently, you'll discover that the spirituality habits provided in this section will be extremely diverse in nature.

Some spiritual habits will include religious habits. Here, I will use words like "God" and "scriptures" due to my Christian background. But readings from the Torah, Quran, I Ching, Book of Mormon, or your preferred religious book are just as valid. Just assume I am talking about the god of your choice when I use these words, not the god of my choice.

Spiritual habits, above all else, are meant to be inclusive, *never* exclusive.

In this section, you'll also discover variations on spiritual habits like:

» Mindfulness habits, which are derivations of Zen Buddhist teachings. These are habits like affirmations, meditation, and breathing exercises.

» Mental well-being habits that are self-directed. These focus on nourishing your "soul" and finding inner peace and happiness.

» Community habits to help others, your community, and even the entire world. They include donating money to worthy causes, volunteering your free time, and mentoring others.

Well, we have a lot to cover, so let's talk about these different spirituality habits.

## #109. Speak Words of Affirmation

**Type:** Support habit

**Best time to complete:** Anytime

**Frequency:** Daily

**Benefit:** If you're unsure about the benefits of affirmations, then here is a list of ways they can improve your mindset. Affirmations:

» **Reduce negative thinking.** By focusing on what's good in your life (and the world around you), you minimize the limiting beliefs that are holding you back.

» **Remind you to appreciate what you have.** You may fail from time to time, but having a daily affirmation like "I am healthy," "I have a family I love," or "I love my job" can remind you of what's truly important to you.

» **Keep you focused on your immediate goals.** If your affirmations tie into the specific outcomes you'd like to accomplish, you'll have a daily reminder of where you should best focus your efforts.

According to Buddha, "What we think, we become." Affirmations are useful because they define our goals, refine our thoughts, and create clear expectations about what you'd like to accomplish.

**Word of warning:** I think affirmations can be a powerful tool, but they do have limits.

You can't sit in your bedroom, recite an affirmation like, "I have enough money in the bank to buy everything I want," and then go buy a flat screen TV. Affirmations are not magic. The "universe" will not magically reward you for your positivity. You will still need to work—and work hard—to get the things you want.

Affirmations are like a hammer—they're just *one tool* you can use to succeed in life.

**Description:** Make eye contact with the mirror as soon as you wake up in the morning. Repeat positive sentences that are personally significant to you aloud four to five times apiece. Here are some examples:

- » *"I am in control of my life."*
- » *"I am worthy of love and joy."*
- » *"I can make a change in this world."*
- » *"I embrace my uniqueness, which makes me beautiful, body and soul."*
- » *"I will accomplish my goals today."*
- » *"I am brimming with energy. I am active and alive."*
- » *"I possess the qualities needed to be successful."*
- » *"Abundance and blessings flow freely through me."*
- » *"Every decision I make is the right one for me."*

» *"I take pleasure and satisfaction in my own solitude."*

» *"I breathe in calmness and breathe out nervousness."*

» *"I let go of my anger so I can see clearly. I am in charge of how I feel."*

There are hundreds and even thousands of affirmations you can use, so my advice is to focus on the phrases that are personally relevant to you. There are three ways to do this.

First, Google search daily affirmations for [goal]. All you have to do is substitute [goal] for the area of your life where you'd like support. So if you want to find affirmations for losing weight, then you'd Google search daily affirmations for weight loss.

The second option is to check out the 101 daily affirmations that Barrie Davenport (my co-author on a few other books) was nice enough to include in the free companion course. Here you'll discover a list of 101 daily affirmations that are broken down into topics like happiness, love and relationships, success, confidence, self-esteem, health, peace, mindfulness, and inner calm.

See it here: liveboldandbloom.com/09/quotes/positive-affirmations.

Finally, you can create your own affirmations, which makes them more personal. Here is a simple, four-step process for doing this:

**1. Create "I am" statements.** These could include "I am healthy" and "I am wealthy." Use simple affirmations that state the positive things about yourself or who you want to be.

**2. Keep it positive.** Affirmations work best when they focus on your goals and eliminate negative thinking. That's why it's important to phrase these statements in a positive and self-confident manner, even if you don't believe the words 100% at first.

**3. Say affirmations in the present tense.** When you talk about goals, it can seem fake to use an affirmation that assumes it is completed. That is why I personally like to focus on affirmations that support the idea that you *can* achieve the goal, instead of having already accomplished it.

For example, if you want to lose 10 pounds, instead of saying an affirmation like "I am at my ideal weight," I'd recommend a phrase like "I have the ability to lose the weight I desire."

**4. Don't worry about how.** Affirmations are about maintaining a positive outlook. This is not the time to worry about how to accomplish your goals.

Well, there you have it: four strategies to create affirmations that directly align with your goals. Just pick one (or all) strategy to create a list of seven to ten statements that you recite during a stack. If you do this habit daily, you'll consistently reinforce the specific outcomes you'd like to achieve in the immediate future.

## #110. Speak Words of Prayer

**Type:** Keystone habit

**Best time to complete:** Anytime

**Frequency:** Daily

**Benefit:** In many ways, prayers are similar to affirmations. You are asking for help to overcome an obstacle for you or an important person in your life. The way prayers are different is because they are backed by faith in your religion. If you're a religious person, then building a prayer habit can become a foundation of your daily routine.

**Description:** The type of praying you do depends on your religion, so the best place to find information would be your local church, temple, or mosque. Here, you can talk to someone who can guide you through what to say and think about during your daily prayers.

Now, if you want an example prayer, I've asked my assistant, Glori, to briefly describe what she does as part of her daily Catholic prayer habit. She writes:

> I didn't pray regularly before, but I started praying daily because I didn't want to pray only in times of need or when I'm in trouble, which was what I was doing. Now, I do it every day because I want to stay in touch and check in with God.
>
> There are two "types" of prayers I regularly pray with my family—the traditional Catholic ones taught by the Church, which we memorize (e.g., praying the rosary, the Angelus, etc.), and personal prayers.
>
> Here's how I pray:
>
> Morning Prayer: I choose to pray every morning before I start work, that way I don't miss it. It helps that I see it on Trello. I pick prayers that are the most relevant to my current priorities: family, work, abundance. I guess in a way, it helps remind me of my "why" and my goals.
>
> It's easy to find prayers online.

Just Google "prayer for [intention]" and edit the prayer if you want.

Night Prayer: I prefer to do the daily examination of conscience. Basically, it's a type of prayer where you're conversing with God about your day. The main parts are thanking God for all blessings, asking for forgiveness, and asking for more help.

Finally, some people prefer the A.C.T.S. acronym (adoration, confession, thanksgiving, supplication), which helps you remember what you should be thinking about while praying."

That's just one example of a faith-based prayer. If you'd like to do something different, then I recommend talking to the people in your religious community to get guidance on what works best for your religion.

## #111. Practice Gratitude

**Type:** Keystone habit

**Best time to complete:** Anytime

**Frequency:** Daily

**Benefit:** It's easy to think that being grateful for what you have in life is something you do for other people. But the main benefit is an internal one. Not only does it make you feel better, but it also helps you become a better person because you'll gain more appreciation for what you already have.

There are many benefits of building the gratitude habit. Here are a few to consider:

» **Gratitude makes us happier.** According to this study, happiness can be increased by as much as 10% by making a daily gratitude list. Incidentally, this is the same amount of happiness increase that comes from doubling your monthly paycheck.

» **Gratitude helps you reach your goals.** According to another study, people who keep gratitude lists are more likely to complete their goals. This is why I'd consider gratitude to be a keystone habit, since it can help you reach desired outcomes in all areas of your life

» **Gratitude makes you a more likeable person**. This study shows that a daily gratitude list can make you more likeable. It increases optimism, self-esteem, and spirituality while decreasing materialism and egocentric tendencies.

» **Gratitude will help you succeed in your career.** Keeping a gratitude list has a big effect on how others perceive you. This increased likeability spills over into your career. People at work are more likely to trust you, which means you'll have a better chance of getting mentors and networking with the top people in your industry.

As you can see, practicing gratitude can lead to many positive benefits in your life, so let's talk about a simple process for adding this habit into your life.

**Description:** Keeping a gratitude list doesn't need to be a formal process. You can write it online, in a journal, or even on a spare scrap of paper. What's important is to think about what (and who) you're thankful for and then write it down *somewhere*.

To get started, I recommend a four-step process:

**1. Be Consistent:** Choose a number of items to be grateful for every day and then stick to this format. It could be one, five, or ten things, but the key thing is to have a number in your mind ahead of time. This is because, throughout the day, your subconscious mind will recognize people and reasons for which you should be thankful.

**2. Be Specific:** Take time to clearly describe why you're grateful for a person, event, or item. Saying, "I am grateful for my wife" doesn't do the trick. You need to come up with a new example from the last couple of days, such as, "I am grateful for my wife, who got up last night to take care of the baby and let me sleep." This is clear and specific and helps you notice the small things that people do for you.

**3. Share your thoughts:** Being grateful to yourself is only half of the job. If you really want to maximize this habit, then express this gratitude to the people who made it happen, like your spouse, boss, friend, coworker, or family member. Saying to your wife, "I appreciate you taking care of the baby last night—I needed that extra sleep," is a great way to strengthen your relationship.

**4. Find the good in the bad:** Not everything in life will be puppies and rainbows, which is why gratitude is important. Instead of looking for the negative in a situation, you can use this habit to look for a positive outcome or an important lesson you learned.

Never underestimate the power of gratitude. By showing appreciation, you'll stop worrying so much about what you're lacking and focus instead on the positive things that you already have.

## #112. Practice Deep Breathing

**Type:** Support habit

**Best time to complete:** Anytime

**Frequency:** Daily

**Benefit:** Deep breathing is like meditation, because it creates a relaxed, calm state of mind. Done correctly, it can be used to relieve the stress that's built up from a hectic workday.

There are a few benefits of practicing deep breathing. First, it clears your negative emotions, which reduces stress, anxiety, and built-up tension. Next, it can improve your health by strengthening your lungs and getting rid of the toxins in your body. Finally, it will improve your mood and increase your energy.

In my opinion, deep breathing is a great habit to do to start your day, *and* an activity you can enjoy in the afternoon to recharge your batteries.

**Description:** Deep breathing is a quick habit that takes less than five minutes to complete. It can be part of a regular stack or a single habit that you do whenever you feel stressed.

Simply follow this nine-step process to get started:

1. Schedule uninterrupted time where you ignore your cell phone or other types of technology.
2. Pick a specific time each day (or a specific stack) where you'll practice deep breathing.
3. Set an alarm for a specific time (like three to five minutes).

4. Sit on a pillow on the floor, in a comfortable chair, or on your couch. Find a comfortable position with your feet on the floor, straighten your back, and rest your hands at your sides.

5. Inhale slowly through your nose until your lungs are filled to capacity.

6. After inhaling as much as possible, hold your breath for a full two seconds.

7. Slowly exhale, in a steady and even manner. If you desire, envision exhaling all your negative emotions.

8. Take a two-second pause.

9. Return to step 5 to repeat this cycle until the alarm signals the end of the session.

Many people don't have time to meditate. If that sounds like you, then you can get some of the same benefits by practicing deep breathing instead. If you follow this nine-step process, you can create a habit that doesn't take long to complete but is great for clearing your mind and relieving anxiety.

## #113. Practice Progressive Relaxation

**Type:** Support habit

**Best time to complete:** Afternoon or evenings

**Frequency:** Daily

**Benefit:** For many, the idea of relaxation is just sitting on your couch in front of the TV. Unfortunately, this doesn't do much to combat the negative effects that stress has on your mind and body. To fight this stress, you can provoke the body's natural way of relaxing by using a technique called "progressive relaxation."

**Description:** You can't completely avoid all stress, but you can reduce it by learning how to naturally make your body rest, which is the opposite of its response to stress.

With progressive relaxation, your:

» Heart rate slows

» Breathing becomes deeper

» Blood pressure stabilizes

» Muscles relax

» Circulation improves

Whenever you feel stressed and need a quick way to relax, try this six-step process:

1. Get comfortable by loosening your clothing.

2. Take a minute to take some slow, deep breaths.

3. Turn your attention to your left foot. Stop to focus on how it feels.

4. Slowly tense the muscles in your left foot as tightly as you can and hold this for ten seconds before relaxing the foot.

5. Pay close attention to the release of tension and how your foot feels as it relaxes. Breathe in at this moment.

6. When you're ready, do this same sequence of tension and relaxation for each area of muscle throughout the body, but don't tense any of your other muscles.

Progressive relaxation is best done in the afternoon or early evening when you've built up stress from a long workday. You can do it as a quick break between tasks or as a five-minute recharge after a particularly grueling part of the day.

## #114. Squeeze a Stress Ball

**Type:** Support habit

**Best time to complete:** Afternoon and evenings

**Frequency:** Daily

**Benefit:** According to a study published in *The Journal of At-Risk Issues*, students who squeezed a stress ball throughout the day had a decrease in their frequency of distraction and an increase in their attention span, leading to better performance in school and greater personal satisfaction.

The act of squeezing a stress ball activates the hand and wrist muscles, and releasing the grip lets the muscles relax. Also, this repeated pattern alleviates tension and boosts blood circulation, which can help give you a quick afternoon pick-me-up.

**Description:** Stress balls are small enough that you can keep them in your desk or in your bag. (Here is one that I recommend from Amazon.)

To properly use a stress ball, try these exercises:

> » Squeeze the ball with your whole hand for a count of three before releasing. Repeat twenty times. Every time you release your muscles, your tension will be released along with your hand.

> » Firmly pinch the ball between each finger individually and your thumb. Go through your fingers one by one on one hand and then switch to the other hand.

> » Twist the stress ball around in one hand at a time. Alternate both the direction of the twisting and the hand to get the full benefits.

These manipulations of the stress ball will help stimulate nerves in your hands that are connected to areas of the brain associated with your emotions. Activating these nerves works similarly to acupressure, where stimulation of one part of the body affects other areas of the body.

## #115. Practice Creative Visualization

**Type:** Support habit

**Best time to complete:** Anytime

**Frequency:** Daily

**Benefit:** Research published in *Neuropsychologia* profiles the many benefits of creative visualization. These studies found that the brain patterns in weightlifters are activated very similarly if they lift hundreds of pounds or if they only imagine lifting an equal amount of weight. Research has also shown that creative visualization is almost as effective as true physical presence, and practicing both is more effective than doing either alone.

**Description:** To help you develop more self-confidence in whatever area of your life it is lacking, follow these five steps to visualize your goal:

1.  **Set the mood.** Find a positive and relaxing area. This may involve going for a quiet walk in a peaceful setting or soaking in your bath—whatever you find to be calming. Once you are relaxed, get comfortable and make sure you are away from any possible disturbances. The longer you can do creative visualization, the better. Try to enter a meditative state before you start by clearing your mind and taking some slow, deep breaths.

2.  **Visualize your goal.** Once you feel calm, create an image of what you want, with as much detail as you would like to include. For example, if you are waiting for an acceptance letter to graduate school, imagine yourself opening that letter at home and visualize the reactions of the people around you when you are accepted. Make this mental movie as realistic as you can.

3.  **Keep those positive feelings.** You are more likely to achieve your goals if you let your visualization experiences influence the other parts of your day. Continue to hold onto the positive feelings of happiness, pride, confidence, and peace that you had when you were visualizing your goal.

4.  **Make this a habit.** Take the time to incorporate creative visualization into your daily routine. Many find it helpful to schedule a specific time to stop what they are doing and work on their power of positive thinking.

5.  **Continue to work hard.** Keep that visualization as a constant motivator to continue going after what you want. The more you get yourself used to this type of positive thinking, the more naturally it will come.

Napoleon Hill once wrote, "Whatever the mind can conceive and believe, it can achieve."

While I don't think you can wish your way to success, I do agree that creative visualization can be a powerful habit when it's combined with consistent, daily effort as you work on your goals.

## #116. Let Go of Regret

**Type:** Support habit

**Best time to complete:** Anytime

**Frequency:** Daily

**Benefit:** It's far too easy to allow your mind to wander off into the past, which often leads to regret and sadness over bad decisions and failed relationships. But if you build a habit of letting go of the past, then you can permanently rid yourself of regret.

**Description:** To let go of regret, you should start by understanding how your mind works and why it's prone to negative thinking. The simplest way to do this is to practice mindfulness.

Mindfulness meditation has been shown to help curb anxiety by reducing the negative thoughts that run through your head. A regular meditation practice is beneficial, but you should also practice mindfulness as you go about your day. Take time to consider things like your movement as you walk and the taste of the food you're eating.

One strategy that I recommend daily is to ask yourself how you're feeling. Even if you aren't worried or depressed, it's important to have regular conferences with yourself to better understand where your thoughts are coming from.

Another idea is to express gratitude for your past. Even when things don't go so well, there is still plenty to be learned. By making mistakes, we can gain wisdom for future scenarios in hopes of not repeating those mistakes.

## #117. Shower Meditation

**Type:** Support habit

**Best time to complete:** Morning

**Frequency:** Daily

**Benefit:** For most people, a shower is already a part of the morning routine. But when you add a quick meditation session to this ritual, you can focus on deep thinking and creating positive thoughts for the day.

Sure, shower mediation might sound hokey, but look it this way: you know how you often get your best thoughts in the shower? Well, the same principle applies here. The calming effect of warm water puts your mind on autopilot, which frees it up to come up with inspirational ideas. (There's even research that shows we often get our best ideas while engaging in mindless tasks, like showering, driving, and doing chores.)

**Description:** Shower meditation can easily be attached to your existing "getting ready" routine. This means you only need to add a few minutes to your shower time to get the full benefit of this habit.

Get started by letting the warm water of the shower wash over your body. Visualize all the stress, anxiety, and worries in your life as being tangible things sticking to your skin. Next, visualize the water and soap scrubbing the stress off your body. Third, envision all the metaphysical "dirt" of your body—your fears, regrets, anxiety, anger, and stress washing free and swirling down the drain. Finally, realize that you are clean, fresh, and ready to start your day free of distractions.

## #118. Practice Mindful Walking

**Type:** Support habit

**Best time to complete:** Anytime

**Frequency:** Daily

**Benefit:** Walking for fitness is best done as part of a regular exercise habit that exceeds thirty minutes. But mindful walking can become a separate habit that combines a *little* fitness with the power of mindfulness. It gives you a mental recharge, gets your blood flowing, and relieves stress. That's why it's the perfect habit for the middle of your workday or during a lunch break.

**Description:** This is best practiced on a slightly long break(s) in your workday. Here's how to get started with mindful walking:

- » Wear comfortable clothing and shoes.
- » Stand still. Become aware of your body and how it feels— your posture, your heels pushing into your shoes, the way you breathe in and out.
- » Bend your knees very slightly and focus on your hips as your center of gravity.

» Begin walking at a slow pace. With each step, feel your leg swinging and your heel, ball, and toe hitting the ground.

» Notice your breathing and walking for five to ten minutes.

» When it's time to end your mindful walking exercise, come to a gentle halt and stand still. Then gradually return to your regular activity.

If you throw in mindful walking to the latter part of the day (or whenever you feel anxiety), you can relieve stress while enjoying nature in a conscious, deliberate manner.

## #119. Practice Aromatherapy

**Type:** Support habit

**Best time to complete:** Anytime

**Frequency:** Daily

**Benefit:** Aromatherapy is using the essential oils of plants to gain physical, mental, or spiritual relief. It has been used widely in Europe as a complementary therapy for over one hundred years.

The purported effects of the oils vary depending on which oil is used (i.e., different oils are thought to have different effects). This means that blending different essential oils can cater to the specific needs of the customer. The different essential oils have different benefits:

» Lavender oil: Stress reliever, antiseptic, antidepressant, anti-inflammatory, decongestant, deodorant, diuretic, and sedative.

» Lemon oil: Reduces cellulite, improves digestion, and reduces headaches and fevers.

» Tea tree oil: Immunity booster that reduces the flu, cold sores, muscle aches, and respiratory issues.

» Cedarwood: A calming agent for stress or anxiety that can also reduce urinary tract infections.

» Bergamot: Helps with stress, depression, anxiety, anorexia, and skin infections (psoriasis and eczema).

» Peppermint: Used for mental alertness *and* for enhancing mood, focus, irritation and redness, congestion, and digestion.

» Chamomile: Calming agent, antibiotic, antiseptic, antidepressant, and overall mood lifter.

» Rose: Helps alleviate depression, anxiety, digestion issues; helps improve circulation, heart problems, and asthma.

» Eucalyptus: Antiseptic, antispasmodic, decongestant, diuretic, stimulant. Also, it reduces migraines, pains, and muscle aches.

» Jasmine: Reduces depression, stress, and addiction issues.

» Patchouli: Decreases anxiety, depression, and fatigue. It also reduces cellulite and bloating.

According to people who strongly believe in the powers of aromatherapy, essential oils work by entering the olfactory system, where they have access to the brain. Once there, they can positively affect your heart rate, blood pressure, breathing, memory, stress levels, and hormone balance.

Now, if all of this sounds too "woo-woo" for you, then you're not alone. While I've dabbled with using essential oils, I can't say with 100% certainty that they actually provide the benefits listed above. Perhaps these results are due to positive thinking by practitioners. But even if some of the claims are nothing more than hype, essential oils are much healthier than the scented candles that most people burn in their homes.

**Description:** There are three different ways to use essential oils, two of which can easily be added to a daily stack.

1. **Aerial Diffusion.** This is the most commonly used method of aromatherapy. The idea behind a diffuser is to mix the essential oils with water, which produces a nice-smelling mist that can permeate a room.

   » There are now some very inexpensive essential oil diffusers (I actually review five different options on my blog).

   » To add this habit to your daily routine, you simply take three to four drops of the essential oil of your choice, add them to a cup of water in your diffuser, set the timer, and then turn the machine on.

   » Once it's ready to go, take a deep breath, relax for a minute or two, and then start your next habit.

2. **Direct Inhalation.** This is a simpler "one-shot" method of using the oils daily. Just open your bottle of essential oil, put it up to your nose, and inhale deeply. You'll find that the oils smell stronger this way, which is perfect if you are using them as a decongestant, disinfectant, or expectorant for your respiratory system.

3. **Topical Application.** This method is something you **don't want to do** as part of a habit stack, but I've included it to completely cover the topic of aromatherapy.

   » This method is generally part of baths, massages, compresses, and therapeutic skin care. If you have ever had a massage, the oils they put on your skin are often some mixture of essential oils designed to help give you relief.

» The reason I don't recommend it here is because topical applications are best used to relieve pain or massage a part of your body. It's a longer habit that can take over thirty minutes to complete, so it's not something that can always fit into your daily routine. (Plus, if you don't know what you're doing and pour an incorrect dosage, you run the risk of causing skin irritation or an allergic reaction.)

## #120. Drink a Calming Beverage (Like Tea)

**Type:** Keystone habit

**Best time to complete:** Anytime

**Frequency:** Daily

**Benefit:** Drinking a calming beverage, like a cup of hot tea, has both physical and mental benefits.

When it comes to your health, drinking tea (specifically green tea) has many detoxifying effects on the body. It has been shown to lower blood pressure, assist hydration (despite the caffeine), and reduce stress hormones.

When it comes to spirituality, a daily tea break gives you "me time," which can be a few spare minutes to think on what has happened during the day and what you plan to do for the next few hours.

**Description:** Start a teakettle right after you wake up as part of your morning habit stack. You can also repeat this habit during the afternoon or at the end of your day.

While the water is boiling, focus on completing two to three tasks in your stack, and then enjoy a few minutes of reflection while you're enjoying a cup of tea.

## #121. Dress for Success

**Type:** Support habit

**Best time to complete:** Anytime

**Frequency:** Daily

**Benefit:** Wearing good clothes not only affects how others see us, it can also affect how we see ourselves. Even if you have a job in a "casual clothing" environment, it's a good habit to dress in clothes that look nice and make you feel confident.

For instance, since I work from home, I can wear whatever I want. This often means my fashion choice is a torn pair of jeans, a hoodie sweatshirt, and a week(s)-long facial hair.

One week, I decided to complete a simple challenge to wear a suit whenever I left the house. I would still go to the same places like I normally did, but I dressed like I was going out for a job interview.

What I noticed during this week-long challenge was a significant boost in my self-confidence and the way people treated me. The lesson I learned here is you can elevate your emotions by looking your best.

**Description:** You don't need to be decked out in a top hat and tuxedo every day to dress for success. Instead, you need to wear clothing that looks good and fits well. (Again, that's why I recommend focusing on buying quality items instead of trying to save money by buying cheap items.)

Here are a few tips you can use to get started:

1. **Make sure you like what you wear.** If necessary, spend a little bit more to purchase truly high-end clothing that you know you'll continue to wear. This is far preferable to cheaper clothing you're less fond of, which is more likely to get worn out quickly.

2. **Purchase clothes that fit.** Even if a suit is your color, it's not going to look any good if it's too tight or too loose on you. If necessary, visit a tailor so he or she can make the proper alterations.

3. **Iron your clothes.** A nice shirt or pants doesn't look nearly as nice if it's smothered with wrinkles. Take time to iron your clothes in the morning. You should also bring your garments to the dry cleaner on a regular basis.

It's amazing to see the difference in responses from people when you look your best. I challenge you to try this habit for a week. Then, if you enjoy this habit, I recommend striving to wear high-quality clothing no matter where you go.

## #122. Practice Random Acts of Kindness

**Type:** Support habit

**Best time to complete:** Anytime

**Frequency:** Daily

**Benefit:** Kindness is contagious. When you do something nice for a stranger for no reason, they feel good and will hopefully pass it on to someone else. Everybody wins, and the world is a slightly better place. That's why you should consider practicing random acts of kindness whenever you're out in the world.

Random acts of kindness are about being a good civic-minded person. It means caring for strangers in the same way you would for friends and family. The best part? It doesn't take much to brighten someone's day. Here's how to do it.

**Description:** The best time for this habit is when you're around other people. So this could be during a commute, while shopping, or when running errands. These are the times when most folks feel hectic and stressed. You can brighten their day a little by committing to at least one act of kindness whenever you're outside your home. All you need to do is look for those opportunities to help others.

This can include:

» Helping an elderly person with their groceries

» Paying for a person's coffee who is behind you in line

» Helping someone whose car is broken down on the side of the road

- » Writing "thank you" notes for public officials, police, and the military

- » Looking for reasons to compliment strangers

- » Helping a lost child find his or her family

- » Seeing someone who looks lost and helping them find their destination

- » Holding doors open for others

- » Asking someone who is crying if there is anything you can do for them

- » Leaving behind random, positive notes to brighten a stranger's day

- » Adding a couple of coins to a parking meter about to expire

- » Keeping your hotel room relatively clean so the maid's job is easier

- » Chiming in with nice things to say about a person when others are spreading gossip

- » Picking up trash and recyclables that you see on the street or in the woods

- » Leaving big tips for a waiter or waitress

- » Printing extra copies of an Internet discount and giving them to people in the store

Also, if you want to see what others are doing and share some of your own experiences with this habit, check out Kindness.org, which is a social media site for people interested in helping others.

If you do small things for others, you make the world a better place while giving yourself the satisfaction that you're helping someone in need.

## #123. Serve Others

**Type:** Support habit

**Best time to complete:** Anytime

**Frequency:** Daily

**Benefit:** If you live or work with others, the daily practice of helping others is something you should consider. Not only will this give you a spiritual boost, but it also gives you an appreciation for the important people in your life.

Another benefit of serving others is that it provides a break from your current troubles. Instead of stressing over a project, you can use your free time to help someone else. This is a great way to increase your morale and level of happiness.

**Description:** Serving others doesn't have to be a massive undertaking. All that's required is to take a few minutes to put someone else first. You could:

» Do a chore that another family member is responsible for, like the laundry, dishes, or taking out the garbage

» Help someone you see struggling with their bags or other items

» Make (or bring) coffee for everyone at work or at home

» Bring in donuts/bagels for the people you work with

» Drive a friend to work

» Make breakfast for your family

» Hold open the door for others until the entire crowd is through the door

» Let others pull in front of you while driving

Based on these examples, you can see that it's not hard to serve others. Sure, these actions might seem insignificant, but doing the small things for other people goes a long way toward making you feel better.

## #124. Schedule a Volunteering Activity

**Type:** Support habit

**Best time to complete:** Anytime

**Frequency:** Weekly or monthly

**Benefit:** As the Dalai Lama once said, "If you want others to be happy, practice compassion. If you want to be happy, practice compassion."

The meaning of this quote is this: When you look for ways to help others and make the world a better place, you will find internal happiness from these actions. A great way to do this is to create a weekly or monthly habit of scheduling a volunteering activity for you and your family.

Here are six benefits of volunteering:

1. **You can leverage your existing skills.** Volunteering doesn't always mean you'll work mindlessly at a soup kitchen, ladling potatoes and carrots onto trays. Instead, you can find volunteer opportunities based on your existing skills that can help others.

   » For instance, if you're good with computers, you could volunteer to teach basic computer skills to the elderly.

This helps others while also solidifying your existing skillset.

2. **You grow as a person.** It can be beneficial to volunteer for projects that help you build skills. Projects like Habitat for Humanity will teach you basic construction skills that you can use for your home. Or even a simple day of volunteering to clear brush from the side of the road can relieve stress from your busy workweek.

3. **You gain appreciation for your free time.** This might seem counterintuitive, but volunteering can create a feeling that you have more time because you'll feel less rushed all the time. In an article published in the Harvard Business Review, Professor Mogilner discovered that people who volunteer feel like they have more time. Their perception of time is that they feel less constrained, stressed, and rushed.

   » To quote Mogilner, "The results show that giving your time to others can make you feel more 'time affluent' and less time-constrained than wasting your time, spending it on yourself, or even getting a windfall of free time."

4. **You build a larger social network.** Volunteering is a great way to meet people. More importantly, you'll connect with people who are thoughtful and care about the welfare of others. Who knows? You may find friends or even romance while sharing your time helping others.

5. **You improve your physical fitness.** Volunteering often involves doing physical activity on your days off. Spending a day outside volunteering is a lot better for your health than

spending the same day indoors, checking email, or watching television.

6. **You help others**. Of course, the most important benefit of volunteering is to help others in your community. The positive impact in other people's lives is something that can never be measured.

As you can see, volunteering can be beneficial in many ways, but it's also an activity that doesn't fit neatly into a regular stack.

My suggestion is to dedicate five to ten minutes each week (or month) to identify upcoming opportunities and schedule them into your calendar. This is similar to how you'd plan a fun activity for you and your family. So, let's talk about how to do that next.

**Description:** One of the biggest barriers to volunteering is uncertainty. You might want to help, but you're unsure about how much time it requires or where to get started. By scheduling an activity in advance, you'll eliminate any excuse for not helping others.

There are three ways to find volunteering opportunities in your immediate area.

First, most local libraries and community centers have posted flyers and advertisements for organizations that need help. If you can't find any, ask a staff member where you can find information about different activities that are coming up.

Next, the Internet is also a good option for finding volunteer opportunities. There are three different websites that I would recommend:

» www.volunteermatch.org
» www.idealist.org/

» www.pointsoflight.org/handsonnetwork

The first two websites are similar to one another. You can search your area by the type of organization or do a search based on a specific skill. The third website only has the option to search by the type of organization you'd like to help.

Finally, you can work with your local church to find volunteering opportunities. Most faith-based groups regularly organize activities where members help others while spreading the word about their religion. You can find information on these activities by attending a service and checking out the weekly bulletins that they hand out.

It's not hard to find volunteering opportunities in your area. Instead of doing it at the last minute, you can set aside time each week to find and schedule an activity.

## #125. Donate to a Charitable Organization

**Type:** Support habit

**Best time to complete:** Anytime

**Frequency:** Monthly

**Benefit:** Like many of the spiritual habits, you can feel better about yourself by looking for ways to help others. One way to do this is to send money to charitable organizations every month. Not only will this provide you with a psychological boost, but it's also a tax-deductible expense.

**Description:** The one concern that many people have about charities is knowing how much money actually goes to those who need it (instead of lining the pockets of the people who run these organizations). Sure, some money needs to be spent on administration fees and to pay the salaries of the workers, but you want to avoid the organizations that charge a high percent of fees.

Fortunately, it's easy to identify the charities that funnel the highest percentage of the money to the people who need it. Every organization must report what they receive in donations and exactly where they spend their money. This makes it simple to figure out where to best focus your charitable donations.

My preferred site for finding this information is GiveWell.org, which focuses on finding the best charities based on four criteria:

1. Effectiveness
2. Cost-effectiveness
3. Transparency
4. Room for more funding

What I like about GiveWell is its simplicity. Instead of using a ranking system like other services, it simply tells you which ones are the best.

That said, if you prefer a ranking system to evaluate a prospective charity, then a good alternative option is Charity Navigator. This site details all the facts on record about the most popular charities, including information like:

» How much they spend on administration (this should be a low percentage unless they have a large staff to promote the charity, like the Red Cross or YMCA)

» How much they spend on advertising

» How much from every donation goes to the direct recipients

» An overall score and rating

My advice is to spend time each month researching a charitable organization that you'll continuously support. Focus on a few groups that align with your personal beliefs and then set up an automatic withdrawal from your account that goes out every month. Then you can use this monthly habit to review these automatic withdrawals to decide if you'd like to maintain this donation or make an adjustment (e.g., increase or decrease the amount you donate).

## #126. Practice Recycling

**Type:** Support habit

**Best time to complete:** Anytime

**Frequency:** Weekly

**Benefit:** Recycling is of tremendous benefit to the environment because it lessens the amount of garbage you're putting into the world. (Plus, it's really easy to do.)

**Description:** Recycling might seem overwhelming at first, but it's just a matter of knowing what can and can't be recycled, then making sure these items are put in the right place. Here are a few pointers to get you started:

» Purchase separate containers for each type of item you'll recycle. Simply call your town to find out what items they accept and then include a bin for each one. This means you could have containers for glass, plastic, aluminum, papers, and cardboard.

» Before you throw away any other item, ask yourself, "Is this recyclable?" If you're not sure, look on Google to get an answer.

» Wash food out of recyclable containers, such as sauce jars. Those who work at the recycling center will appreciate you taking the time to remove the food, which can spoil quickly and become repulsive.

» Hold onto items that still have some use. Recycling is all about reusing things, and this can start at home. If you wash out a jar and realize that it's the perfect size to store loose change, then hold onto it. Not only are you helping the environment, but you're also saving money on new jars.

» See how much you can recycle each week. If your garbage output is much higher than your recycling output, think about how you can change this so that you recycle more than you throw away.

Recycling is just one action you can do to reduce the environmental impact that you and your family have on the world. Sure, it requires a time *and* financial investment, but it is a small sacrifice to make the world better for future generations.

## #127. Commit to Conservation-Friendly Activities

**Type:** Support habit

**Best time to complete:** Anytime

**Frequency:** Daily

**Benefit:** Another way to positively impact the environment is to make changes on a personal level. While we can't be expected to all go off the grid and live in mud houses, changing a few wasteful habits in your day-to-day life is a great way to show your appreciation for the environment and the natural resources that we all depend upon.

**Description:** Being conservation-friendly is just as much a matter of undoing bad habits as it is doing good habits. When you go about your day, take a moment to consider the environmental impact of your decisions and what you can do to lessen it, such as:

» **Taking shorter showers.** People use 80–100 gallons of water a day on average, and much of that comes from our showers. Set a timer for five minutes or less for your showers.

» **Unplugging electronics when you're not using them.** Even if your television is turned off, it's still consuming power through being plugged in. Simply take a moment to get up and unplug it after turning it off.

» **Using reusable bags when shopping.** A canvas shopping bag is much better for the environment than a paper or plastic one, and is also more durable and holds many more groceries.

» **Eating less meat.** Preparing livestock animals for meat has a huge impact on the environment. By going without meat for at least one meal a day, you are reducing your carbon footprint.

» **Limiting car usage.** Driving a car everywhere you go has a substantial impact on the environment and is sometimes unnecessary. If somewhere you need to go is close enough, take the time to walk or bike instead of driving.

This handful of habits can have a positive long-term impact on the planet. By thinking carefully about what you do daily, you can take a few tiny steps to reducing your carbon footprint.

# PART XII

## BUILDING LIFELONG
## HABIT STACKS

# 9 Example Habit Stacking Routines

At this point, you know how to build a habit stack and you've reviewed the 127 habits that can be added to a routine. But what you *might not know* is how to put these actions into a simple framework. In this section, you'll discover nine example stacks that best demonstrate how this concept would work in your life.

Before we get started, I want to remind you that the following are just examples. At no point should you feel like you "need" to complete any (or all) of the suggested habits. Instead, use them as a launching pad for possible ideas.

## Example 1: Morning Routine Stack

**Total Time:** 40 to 50 minutes

A morning routine can help you shake off that groggy feeling when you first wake up and get you ready to attack the day in an energized state. That's why I recommend a series of habits that focus on health, mindfulness, and planning your schedule.

» Fill a thirty-two-ounce water bottle (habit #45)

» Prepare a smoothie drink (habit #44)

» Take daily vitamins (habit #43)

» Complete a seven-minute workout (habit #48)

» Review your goals (habit #3)

» Identify your three most important tasks (habit #2)

» Read a book chapter (habit #63)

» Meditate (habit #53) *or* do shower meditation (habit #117)

- » Pack a meal, snack, and coffee (habit #28)
- » Leave a caring note (habit #97)

## Example 2: Lunch Break Stack

**Total Time:** 45 minutes

Your mind (and body) requires a break after working for a few hours. You could do what most people do during their lunchtime: eat, chat with friends, and browse the Internet. But a better use of this time is to grab a quick bite and practice a few habits that will provide an energetic boost when you need it the most.

- » Get outside (habit #69)
- » Practice mindful walking (habit #118)
- » Practice progressive relaxation (habit #113)
- » Complete a "deskercise" routine (habit #50)
- » Clean your office desk (habit #82)
- » Drink a calming beverage (like tea) (habit #120)
- » Read a book chapter (habit #63)

## Example 3: Evening Stack

The way you end each day sets the tone for your productivity and attitude when you arrive at work the next morning. The following habits can help you finish the workday on a high note. (Plus, you can complete a few more habits when you arrive home that will prepare you for yet another successful day.)

**Total Time:** 20 minutes (at work) + 25 minutes (at home)

## AT WORK:

- » Track time for your activities (habit #12)
- » Write a "done list" (habit #14)
- » Clean your office desk (habit #82)
- » Practice self-education on the drive home (habit #61)

## AT HOME:

- » Put away three items (habit #80)
- » Plan a morning "getting out the door" routine (habit #89)
- » Maintain a food journal (habit #41)
- » Enjoy a distraction (habit #74)
- » Follow a "shut down" routine (habit #54)
- » Use the sleep cycle app (habit #55)

### Example 4: Productivity Stack

Productivity isn't measured by the number of hours you work—it's measured by the *quality* of the tasks you've completed. A simple way to improve your career success is to structure your days so that you work on important tasks in your most energetic, motivated state. The following productivity habits can make that happen.

**Total Time:** 26 minutes

- » Create an interruption-free environment (habit #7)
- » Identify your three most important tasks (habit #2)
- » Do the hardest task first (habit #4)
- » Improve focus by playing music (habit #9)
- » Track time for your activities (habit #12)

» Work in Pomodoro blocks (habit #13)

» Reward yourself for completing a task (habit #11)

» Write a "done list" (habit #14)

## Example 5: Gym Stack

Sometimes the little things can make or break your commitment to a habit. This is especially true when it comes to exercising. It's far too easy to skip a day when the weather isn't cooperating or you don't have the right equipment. But if you follow this stack (in conjunction with a regular exercise habit), you will eliminate every excuse to miss a workout.

**Total Time:** 19 minutes

» Follow a "getting out the door" routine in the evening (habit #89)

» Connect your location to Beeminder (habit #56)

» Complete your workout

» Increase your flexibility (habit #51)

» Weigh yourself (habit #40)

» Track your workout in a journal

## Example 6: Weight Loss Stack

Creating a permanent weight change doesn't happen by following the latest fad diet. It comes from building small habits that encourage positive behavior. If you add the following stack to your day, you'll create subconscious changes that will result in a slow but consistent loss of weight.

**Total Time:** 35 to 40 minutes (weekly) + 5 to 15 minutes (daily)

## WEEKLY:

> » Plan your meals (habit #32)

> » Prepare a food shopping list (habit #33)

## DAILY:

> » Maintain a food journal (habit #41)

> » Replace one food item (habit #42)

> » Fill a 32-ounce water bottle (habit #45)

> » Wear a step-tracking device (habit #46)

> » Walk between blocks of focused effort (habit #47)

> » Connect your location to Beeminder (habit #56)

> » Weigh yourself (habit #40)

### Example 7: Dating Stack

**Total Time:** 5 to 10 minutes (weekly) + 22 minutes (daily)

Your dating life should include more activity than scrolling through an app, swiping left and right. If you want to find the perfect match, then you need to put yourself out there … *you know* … in the real world.

A few ways to do this is to focus on what you enjoy, increase your social network, and become a well-rounded person who *naturally* attracts others. The following habits will help you expand your network while providing opportunities to enjoy fun with friends and your dates.

## WEEKLY:

> » Research a fun activity (habit #102)

## DAILY:

> » Dress for success (habit #121)

> » Do an activity that makes you happy (habit #91)

> » Introduce yourself to someone new (habit #92)

> » Contact one person on a dating site (habit #93)

> » Give a compliment (habit #94)

### Example 8: Weekly Stack

**Total Time:** 81 minutes

There are many activities you can do weekly to have a well-rounded life. My suggestion is to set aside at least an hour (preferably on a Sunday) to plan the next seven days.

Here you'll review important personal obligations, schedule activities that can be shared with friends and family, and then map out your work projects. The following habits can help you get started.

> » Perform a safety check (habit #60)

> » Chunk down a project (or task) into manageable steps (habit #5)

> » Identify one task to delegate or outsource (habit #15)

> » File away loose paperwork (habit #83)

> » Check your billing statements (habit #24)

> » Plan your meals (habit #32)

> » Prepare a food shopping list (and stick to it!) (habit #33)

» Add to your "bucket list" (habit #71)

» Add to your "soon list" (habit #72)

» Schedule a volunteering activity (habit #124)

## Example 9: Power Stack

**Total Time:** 60 minutes

A power stack is simply a combination of the best habits that will have the biggest impact on your life. The idea here is to identify the habits that most successful people complete and then do them daily—preferably first thing in the morning.

The habits you choose are up to you, but the best example of a power stack can found in *The Miracle Morning* by Hal Elrod.

What Hal recommends is the S.A.V.E.R.S. formula, which stands for silence, affirmations, visualization, exercise, reading, scribing. Each takes ten minutes to complete, which totals an hour of effort. If you'd like to put Hal's idea into practice, then the following is a *very* brief overview of the stack that he recommends.

» **Silence:** Meditation, prayer, or breathing to block out the "daily noise" and calm your mind.

» **Affirmations:** Encouraging words that focus on your goals and habits.

» **Visualization:** Creating a mental movie where you walk through your goals and picture what it's like to achieve them.

» **Exercise:** Simple, quick workouts that get the blood flowing and elevate your mood.

» **Reading:** Going through high-value, nonfiction books related to your goals, or anything that enriches your daily existence.

» **Scribing:** Journaling as a way to express your thoughts and think through the current challenges you are facing.

These are just nine examples of habit stacks. However, the options (and the combinations Of habits) are limitless. That's why I encourage you to cherry-pick the ones that look interesting to you and then ignore everything else.

To get started, think about your immediate goals and the specific actions you need to accomplish daily to make them happen. Whatever sticks out in your mind are the habits that will become part of your next stack.

Now, I'll admit that this is an idealistic view of habit stacking. As much as I'd like to think everything will go perfectly for you, I'm also a realist. I know there *will* be times when you encounter challenges— even disruptions—to your routine. That's why it's important to plan for these situations and know what to do when they occur.

Let's talk about that in the next section.

# 6 Challenges That Might Be Holding You Back

We all occasionally struggle when it comes to building habits. You read about an exciting way to improve your life, but then after doing it for a few days you quickly realize that it's a lot harder than you originally thought. What usually happens then is you quit in frustration because you simply can't maintain this new habit.

People often give up *not because they're lazy*, but because they don't know how to overcome specific events and challenges. Something comes up in their lives that interrupts their habits, and then they don't know how to "get back on that horse after they have fallen off."

I feel the key to consistency with *any* type of habit is to plan ahead for the common challenges that will interrupt your routine. In this section, we'll go over six limiting beliefs that might prevent you from success:

1. "I don't feel motivated to get started."
2. "I don't have enough time for habit stacking."
3. "I often get distracted and forget about habit stacking."
4. "I have better things to do with my time."
5. "It's too easy to skip this routine."
6. "I often get derailed by life events."

As you start to incorporate habit stacking into your life, you will experience the occasional challenge. That's why I recommend reading this section *at least* once, and then bookmarking it as a reference for those times when you struggle with your routines.

## Challenge #1: "I don't feel motivated to get started."

You have a stack scheduled and you have the checklist in front of you, but you simply don't feel motivated to get started. In fact, you can think of a few dozen other things you'd rather do than complete this routine.

Trust me, you're not alone here. Many people struggle with their habits. This is true *even* for the permanent routines that you've completed a thousand times before.

As I've mentioned before, I try to run a marathon twice a year, which means I must do *a lot* of running each week—usually in a variety of environments that are not particularly pleasant. Sometimes it's too hot. Or cold. Or rainy. Or dark. Or boring (if I have to run on a treadmill at the gym).

In fact, I feel like I *don't want to run* about 50% of the time. Yet, I force myself to get started by doing a little bit of "creative lying." Whenever I feel a lack of motivation, I tell myself to "just run a mile or two, then see how you feel."

What usually happens is, after I get to the second mile, I'll feel energized enough to run a few more, and usually this is enough to get me through the workout.

You can apply creative lying to your habit stacking routine whenever you feel a lack of motivation. In fact, I recommend a simple solution that you can apply to any hard-to-start routine. It's called mini habits, which I mentioned in a previous section.

## Mini Habits: The Solution to Getting Started

*Mini habits* is a term coined by my friend Stephen Guise, in the book of the same name. (There is also a similar concept called *Tiny Habits*, which is a phrase created by BJ Fogg.)

The purpose of mini habits is to remove the resistance that you feel when it comes to starting a difficult (or time-consuming) task. It's easy to schedule an activity into your day (like running for an hour), but it's hard to complete when you feel a lack of interest.

Mini habits work because they eliminate motivation from the equation. Instead of setting an extremely challenging goal, you set a "lowball" goal that makes it super simple to get started.

Let's go over a quick scenario to illustrate this point:

Imagine you set a goal to exercise for thirty minutes. Everything goes perfectly the first week. You join a gym, attend a few classes, and enjoy the endorphin rush of frequent exercise.

One day, your boss asks you to work late, so you're forced to skip your scheduled class. You tell yourself, "That's okay, I'll do it tomorrow." But in the back of your mind, you start to doubt your commitment to this new exercise habit.

This pattern repeats itself over the next few weeks. You miss classes for a variety of reasons: Your kid has the flu. You didn't pack your gym clothes. The roads are covered in snow. You have to wash your cat. Suddenly, this "thirty minutes of exercise time" has turned into a task that feels impossible to do consistently. Stinks, doesn't it?

The mini habit concept prevents this scenario because it eliminates that overwhelmed feeling you get when you think a task is too difficult to complete.

To quote Stephen:

> When people try to change, they usually try to get amped up for the change, but no matter how badly you want the change, you haven't changed yet! As motivation wanes, so does progress. *You don't need more motivation, you need a strategy that can leverage the abilities of the current you into a better you.*

In other words, the simplest, most effective way to create a lasting change is to create a goal that might seem too easy to complete but is also so easy that you can do it on a consistent basis.

### Example: Stephen's "One Push-up Challenge"

Stephen discovered the concept of mini habits through something he calls his "One Push-up Challenge." For a long time, he relied too much on willpower and motivation to get inspired to exercise. Then, one day, he decided to set a very easy goal—**commit to completing one single push-up.** If he wanted to do more, then he would, but the most important thing was to set a goal that was incredibly simple to achieve.

The number of push-ups is irrelevant. What was crucial was the fact that he was building a habit. No matter what happened during the day, he completed the push-up goal for that day.

To quote Stephen:

> Daily exercise in small amounts is far more powerful than single, intense workout sessions. The former can become habit

and destroy your resistance over time, while the latter makes you really sore for a few days and that's about it. When my resistance to exercise had been whittled down, I began my current streak of going to the gym 3–6x a week. I haven't looked back.

There are five reasons why the mini habits concept can help you stick with a habit stacking routine:

1. **Your success will lead to more success.** It's easy to get discouraged when you fail repeatedly. On the other hand, a mini habit will create a sense of excitement because you're achieving an important daily goal. Trust me—when you have a thirty-day streak going, it's easier to feel that excitement to get started each day.

2. **You will avoid the guilt trip.** It's fun to have a streak of consecutive days where you work at something new. This is the exact opposite of what happens when you miss a day or two. There is nothing to be gained by setting an overly ambitious goal. All this does is create a negative attitude toward an activity that's supposed to be fun.

3. **You increase the desire to build the habit.** It's easy to procrastinate when you know that every day you "must" spend *hours* on a task. In fact, you'll quickly learn to dread this activity. But by setting an achievable goal, you push past that inertia and get started because the goal seems completely doable.

4. **You'll do more than planned.** A strange thing happens once you overcome your initial inertia and get started. What usually happens is you convince yourself to keep going and

do way more than you'd planned. You're using the power of self-deception to trick yourself into getting started. This creates enough momentum that you'll keep going long after you've passed the daily goal.

5. **You'll form a habit.** Consistency is more important for building habits than hitting a specific metric. At first, an external cue will trigger your routine, like an alarm on your phone. But eventually, you'll simply remember to work at your skill at a specific time each day. This is what happens when you build a positive habit into your life.

## How to Apply Mini Habits to Habit Stacking

I recommend creating a mini habit where you can complete your stacks no matter what comes up in your life. Since most people get tripped up by the amount of effort required to complete this routine, you should make the commitment as brain-dead-simple as possible to get started.

For instance, you create a mini habit goal like:

> » Completing *just* the first small action
>
> » Telling yourself that you'll only do half the habits
>
> » Reducing the time for the longer habits
>
> » Skipping the habits that you truly dread
>
> » Telling yourself you'll quit when you get bored

I recognize that these tips seem counterintuitive to the rules described in Part IV. But sometimes, when you're feeling a lack of motivation, you need an extra push to spur you into action. Creating a mini habits goal can be that push. It will prevent those times when you'll skip a routine because you think it's too overwhelming.

Sure, there will be days when you can't complete a full stack. But what's important (as you've heard me mention already) is to stay consistent with doing something every single day.

## Challenge #2: "I don't have enough time for habit stacking."

Sometimes you feel like you're too busy to squeeze in time for a new habit. This can be especially true if you schedule it in the evening, after you've already had a busy, stressful day. I'm not going to lie and say it's always easy to carve out a spare thirty minutes, but there are two strategies you can use to "find" more time.

### First, Say No to Certain Activities

Right now, there are probably a few activities that can be streamlined or even eliminated from your schedule. Perhaps you could skip a half hour of TV time. Or find a creative way to skip that low-value meeting that isn't important for your job. Or maybe you could bring a bag lunch to work, eat at your desk, and complete a stack during your lunch break.

My point is simple: you probably waste more time than you think. The obvious culprit is media consumption. It has been reported that the average US citizen spends eight hours daily consuming media, including watching television and surfing the Internet. If you do both activities, that's a *quarter* of your day spent doing nothing. If you can sacrifice just an hour of this time, that's one more hour than most people spend on their goals.

### Second, Wake up Earlier

If you want to build a positive habit stacking routine, then it's worth getting up earlier in the morning when there are fewer distractions. Now, this doesn't have to mean you'll lose sleep. In fact, if you go to bed thirty minutes earlier at night (maybe by skipping one TV show), then you'll feel just as rested when you get up in the morning.

Just do the math: 30 minutes each day is an extra 210 minutes (or 3 hours 40 minutes) each week. Over a year's time, that's 182.5 hours that can be dedicated to deliberate practice. I guarantee this small change will give you enough time to have an amazing impact.

Don't make the excuse that you don't have enough time to work on a positive habit. If you have enough time to goof off and consume hours of media, then you absolutely have time to work on your personal development.

### Challenge #3: "I often get distracted and forget about habit stacking."

Sometimes "life" will intrude upon your attempts at personal development. Okay, who am I kidding? Not sometimes—nearly *all* of the time.

You probably feel that it's nearly impossible to make any plan without it getting disrupted. These distractions often seem relentless, especially the moment you decide to work on self-improvement.

These plan destroyers include:

» Impulses to work on something else

» Temptations to goof off with your cell phone, surf the Internet, or watch a TV show

» Children who need attention, or family members who are sick

» Inclement weather

» Work problems

» Relationship trouble

» Vacations

» General "stuff happens" situations

Here's the thing: *No one* can build positive habits in a vacuum, free from responsibilities and disruptions.

It's not like everyone in your life will suddenly need less from you the moment you decide to work on yourself. But, if you are smart about how you structure your day, and if you maintain open communication with others, it's not that hard to manage these potential disruptions.

There are numerous strategies you can use to prevent distractions from derailing your habit stacking efforts. Here are seven ideas:

1. Wake up before anyone else and complete the routine first thing in the morning. Most people won't be up, so this virtually eliminates all potential people distractions.

2. Understand your bad triggers, which cause you to procrastinate or make you feel unmotivated. Keeping track of your negative habits will help you identify those moments of weaknesses when you are likely to skip the routine.

3. Create an "if-then plan" related to your biggest distractions. For instance, if you know your husband often interrupts your

routine, then create a strategy of how to prevent or deal with the situation.

4. Complete the routine in a part of your home that family members don't typically use (like your basement).

5. Avoid all forms of technology in the 15 minutes before the routine (i.e., cell phone, laptop, and TV), because this will remove the temptation to goof off or focus on work projects.

6. Make a promise that you'll "treat yourself" to a reward right after you complete a stack.

7. Schedule this habit into your day like an appointment. Let friends, family, and coworkers know that this is a sacred time that shouldn't be interrupted *unless* it's an emergency.

None of these strategies work 100% of the time. But if you proactively address your distractions on a continual basis, you'll find that it's not hard to slowly eliminate them from your life.

## Challenge #4: "I have better things to do with my time."

I'll admit it: Sometimes habit stacking can feel like a grind. You wake up in the morning, knowing you have dozens of tasks or errands to complete, so the last thing you want to do is to "waste time" on an activity that doesn't have a positive, immediate benefit.

That said, if you constantly dread this activity or feel like it's a big waste of your time, then I suggest that you examine the "why" behind your desire to complete this routine.

Odds are, a negative feeling is the result of not aligning each habit with one of your goals.

**Stick to Your Top Five Priorities**

Here's a brief story that best illustrates the importance of knowing and sticking to your priorities. This was first shared by Scott Dinsmore on his Live Your Legend site.

Here he talked about meeting a friend of Warren Buffett's pilot (whom he calls Steve).

In this conversation, Steve talked about how Buffett encouraged him to write down a list of twenty-five things he wanted to do over the next few years. After completing this list, Buffett told him to review this list and circle his top five priorities. These goals would be more important than anything else in Steve's life.

Next, Steve was encouraged to create an action plan for these five activities. Buffett encouraged him to write them down as actionable goals and then get started on them immediately.

Toward the end of this conversation, Buffett asked a simple question: "But what about these other twenty things on your list that you didn't circle? What is your plan for completing those?"

Steve's reply was probably what most of us would say: "Well, the top five are my primary focus, but the other twenty come in at a close second. They are still important, so I'll work on those intermittently as I see fit as I'm getting through my top five. They are not as urgent, but I still plan to give them dedicated effort."

**Buffett's reply was surprising:** "No. You've got it wrong, Steve. Everything you didn't circle just became your *'avoid at all costs' list*. No matter what, these things get no attention from you until you've succeeded with your top five."

Great advice, right?

Especially since it comes from one of the wealthiest people in the world.

**Build a Habit Stack Around Important Goals**

The lesson here is that while we live in an amazing world full of opportunities, it's risky to try to do it all. If you're trying to balance a dozen projects and obligations, then you'll make very little progress with any one of them.

My advice is simple—in fact, it matches the advice shared by Warren Buffett:

» Write down a list of twenty-five priorities that you want to accomplish in the next few years.

» Identify the top five that are important *right now*.

» Identify the other twenty that might be a distraction from your five priorities. Make a mental commitment to avoid these activities at all costs.

» If you feel disinterested in a stacking routine, then closely examine *each* of the habits. If you don't have a clear reason why an action is important, then get rid of it!

We *all* feel the occasional lack of desire. Often, you might think there are better things to do with your time. But if each habit directly relates to a major goal, then all you need to do is remind yourself why you've chosen to complete these daily actions.

## Challenge #5: "It's too easy to skip this routine."

People often procrastinate (or avoid) a habit when there is no immediate negative consequence. Sure, you know it's important to improve your health, finances, and relationships, but these often don't seem as urgent as the next coming project.

I feel this challenge is the direct result of nobody holding you accountable for skipping this routine. Fortunately, it's not hard to overcome this challenge. All you need to do is **work with an accountability partner**.

An accountability partnership is an arrangement where two (or more) people mutually agree to support one another in the achievement of a specific goal. The two of you should have daily or weekly feedback sessions to share wins and talk about your current challenges.

In regard to habit stacking, your partner will keep you on track to make sure you don't skip this routine. And when you do, it's up to this person to help you make sure you don't miss another one. This feedback can be given in a friendly manner, but the point of accountability is to make sure both people follow through with their commitments.

The main benefit of accountability is that you can talk about your specific issues with someone who understands what you're going through. In fact, you can use this concept for any goal related to the following:

» Fitness training

» Building a business

» Diet or nutrition

» Positive self-talk or emotional growth

» Effective communication

» Relationships

» Parenting

» Smoking cessation

» Budgeting (stop wasting money or start saving)

» Home organization or cleaning

» Writing

If working with an accountability partner sounds like something you want to do, then you should understand both the advantages and disadvantages of this arrangement.

**Advantages:**

» You have an opportunity to coach someone while also receiving value in return.

» You get a very direct form of accountability. Habit-building apps are impersonal, but forming a partnership with someone can lead to a strong friendship as you share your hopes, struggles, dreams, and goals with each other.

» You connect at a mutually convenient time. There are no appointments like you would have with a professional coach.

» Accountability partnerships are usually free.

**Disadvantages:**

» You won't always be compatible with the person you pick. If you clash with your accountability partner, you are likely to have arguments or major disagreements. This can be a discouraging experience, or even become a major obstacle that gets in the way of your goals.

» This type of relationship is difficult to maintain if you are both busy and don't have similar schedules.

» If one accountability partner is at a higher level than the other, the coaching can be very one-sided.

» It's not as formal as other types of accountability, which can be a distraction if you have a results-driven personality.

Working with an accountability partner is a great option if you need constant feedback on your goals. If you're interested in finding someone to partner with, then I recommend joining our habits-focused Facebook Group and asking around for an accountability partner there: www.HabitsGroup.com.

## Challenge #6: "I often get derailed by life events."

It's easy to fall off the habit wagon. You're consistent for a few weeks, but then your schedule is thrown into disarray because of a vacation, emergency, or holiday (like Thanksgiving or Christmas). Next thing you know, this small hiccup has turned into a streak of missed days. Even worse, you play the "blame game," where you use negative self-talk and get mad at yourself because you can't stick with a new habit.

Trust me: the scenario I just described happens to *all of us*.

Fortunately, there are two simple strategies you can use to reignite your dedication to a habit stack.

**First, you need to forgive yourself.** Understand that everyone slips up from time to time and nobody is 100% perfect with their habits.

Beating yourself up for missing a few days, or even a week, accomplishes nothing.

My advice: take responsibility for slipping up, but also forgive yourself. Honestly, it's not the end of the world if you skip the occasional day.

**Next, "get back on the horse" by restarting your stack.** The key here (as you probably guessed) is consistency. It's better to have a streak of completed days than it is to complete a dozen habits one day, then skip the next day. Just focus on completing one to three small actions for a few days and then add more once the routine becomes a permanent behavior.

Well, these are the six challenges that you might face when building a permanent routine. If you follow my advice, then you'll discover it's not hard to overcome the occasional obstacle that comes your way.

# Habit Stacking (a Quick Recap)

We have covered a wealth of information throughout this book, so at this point, you might be unsure about how (or where) to get started. That's why I'd like to close out this book with a quick recap of the critical thirteen steps you can use as a blueprint for getting started with habit stacking:

1. Identify an area of your life you want to improve, and start with a five-minute block of habits. This will help you create consistency by making sure that you're sticking with this new routine.

2. Focus on small wins by picking simple habits that don't require much willpower, like taking a vitamin, weighing yourself, or reviewing your goals. Complete these activities for a week or two until the stack is automatic, then add more habits.

3. Remember: Even though there are 127 habits mentioned in this book, you only need to pick a few to create a positive change in your life.

4. Pick a time, location, or combination of both for when you'll complete this routine. (Also, be sure to review the nine example routines mentioned earlier in this section.)

5. Anchor your stack to a trigger, which is an existing habit that you automatically do *every* day, like showering, brushing your teeth, checking your phone, going to the refrigerator, or sitting down at your desk. This is important because you need to be 100% certain that you won't miss this trigger.

6. Create a logical checklist, which should include the sequence of the actions, how long it takes to complete each item, and where you'll do them.

7. Be accountable by using an app like Coach.me to track your progress and frequently talking to an accountability partner with whom you share your breakthroughs, challenges, and future plans.

8. Create small enjoyable rewards that help you stick with this routine and hit important milestones. These rewards can include watching your favorite TV show, eating a healthy snack, or relaxing for a few minutes.

9. Focus on repetition by never missing a day. In fact, it's crucial that you stick to the routine—even if you need to skip one or two habits. Consistency is more important than anything else.

10. Avoid breaking the chain by eliminating any excuse for missing a day. Create a doable daily goal that can be achieved no matter what happens, and don't let yourself be talked out of it. Perhaps you'll set a small goal requiring you to only complete two or three actions. The important thing is to set a goal that can be achieved even when you have an off day.

11. Expect the occasional challenge or setback. In fact, it's better if you assume they will happen and then make a plan for how you'll handle them. If you get stuck, review the six challenges that we just covered and implement the advice for your unique obstacle.

12. Schedule the frequency of a stack by committing to this routine as a daily, weekly, or monthly series of actions. My suggestion is to get started with a simple daily routine, but

when you want to build more habits, add a weekly or monthly task.

13. Scale up your stack by adding more habits and increasing the total time of the routine. But be very cautious with this step. If you notice that it's getting progressively harder to get started (e.g., you're procrastinating), then either reduce the number of habits or ask yourself *why* you want to skip a day. The more you understand about your lack of motivation, the easier it will be to overcome it.

14. Build one routine at a time because each additional new routine increases the difficultly of sticking with your current habits. Only when *you* feel that a stack has become a permanent behavior should you consider adding a new routine.

That's it—thirteen steps to build a stack that will create a positive, long-term change in your life. I won't lie and say it'll be easy 100% of the time, but if you stick to these steps, then you can overcome any challenge that comes your way.

# Final Thoughts on Habit Stacking

Our time together is almost complete.

I'll admit that many of the habit suggestions we've covered aren't revolutionary ideas. You already know it's important to eat healthy foods, exercise more, focus on critical tasks, and review your goals. Odds are, you've heard this advice a million times before.

But what you might not have realized is the power of consciously scheduling these activities into your day and creating a framework allowing you to be 100% confident that you'll complete each task— *every day*—without fail.

Now, as we close things out, I want to remind you of a simple rule:

**If you want to improve your life, take a close look at your goals and find the one area where you need the most help.** Whatever you pick should become part of your first stack.

*Do you wake up in the morning feeling groggy and unmotivated?*

Then build a morning stack that combines health, spirituality, and career habits that will give you an energized start to the day.

*Are you struggling with getting things done at work?*

Then start your workday by focusing on the habits that will have the biggest impact on your job performance. In addition, be sure to include the habits where you track your time in order to minimize (or eliminate) the distractions that often prevent you from doing important work.

*Do you waste time at night before going to sleep?*

Then build a small stack where you enjoy fun, distracting activities in the few hours before bedtime. Then, in the last hour, strictly follow a "shut down" routine, and finish off by using the Sleep Cycle app to closely monitor your sleep patterns.

As you can see, **the habit-stacking framework is flexible and can easily fit into any busy schedule**. To get started, all you need to do is identify an area of your life you'd like to improve and have the willingness to make it happen.

Now it's up to you.

I encourage you to *not* just close this book. Instead, I encourage you to use the thirteen-step plan to turn this information into action. Just pick a time of day and then schedule it into your routine. (As always, if you get stuck, you can check out the free companion website, which is full of tools that can help you get started.)

Once you're comfortable with a routine, add a second routine and then a third. Rinse and repeat until you're completing dozens of small habits *every day*—all helping you live life to the fullest.

I wish you the best of luck.

Steve "S.J." Scott

# One Last Reminder ...

We've covered a wealth of information in this book, but that doesn't mean your self-educational efforts should end here. In fact, I've created a small companion website that includes many resources mentioned throughout *Habit Stacking*.

Here are just a few things I've included:

- » The Habit Stacking Quick Start Guide, which is a printable reference guide of all the rules, steps and a list of the 127 habits
- » Each link and resource mentioned in this book, broken down into 12 sections.
- » The Todoist walkthrough video
- » The Facebook Group walkthrough video
- » A visual walkthrough of the ATimeLogger productivity apps.
- » A list of 155 ways to reward yourself for accomplishing a goal or task.

Plus, I will be adding more goodies to this website in the months to come. So, if you're interested in expanding on what you've learned in this book, then click this link and join us today:

www.developgoodhabits.com/stacking_website

# Thank You!

Before you go, we'd like to say thank you for purchasing my book.

You could have picked from dozens of books on habit development, but you took a chance and checked out this one.

So, big thanks for downloading this book and reading all the way to the end.

Now we'd like ask for a small favor. Could you please take a minute or two and leave a review for this book on Amazon?

This feedback will help us continue to write the kind of Kindle books that help you get results. And if you loved it, please let us know 😊

# More Books by Steve

» Novice to Expert: 6 Steps to Learn Anything, Increase Your Knowledge, and Master New Skills

» Declutter Your Mind: How to Stop Worrying, Relieve Anxiety, and Eliminate Negative Thinking

» The Miracle Morning for Writers: How to Build a Writing Ritual That Increases Your Impact and Your Income

» 10-Minute Digital Declutter: The Simple Habit to Eliminate Technology Overload

» 10-Minute Declutter: The Stress-Free Habit for Simplifying Your Home

» The Accountability Manifesto: How Accountability Helps You Stick to Goals

» Confident You: An Introvert's Guide to Success in Life and Business

» Exercise Every Day: 32 Tactics for Building the Exercise Habit (Even If You Hate Working Out)

» The Daily Entrepreneur: 33 Success Habits for Small Business Owners, Freelancers and Aspiring 9-to-5 Escape Artists

» Master Evernote: The Unofficial Guide to Organizing Your Life with Evernote (Plus 75 Ideas for Getting Started)

» Bad Habits No More: 25 Steps to Break Any Bad Habit

» Habit Stacking: 97 Small Life Changes That Take Five Minutes or Less

» To-Do List Makeover: A Simple Guide to Getting the Important Things Done

» 23 Anti-Procrastination Habits: How to Stop Being Lazy and Get Results in Your Life

» S.M.A.R.T. Goals Made Simple: 10 Steps to Master Your Personal and Career Goals

» 115 Productivity Apps to Maximize Your Time: Apps for iPhone, iPad, Android, Kindle Fire and PC/iOS Desktop Computers

» Writing Habit Mastery: How to Write 2,000 Words a Day and Forever Cure Writer's Block

» Daily Inbox Zero: 9 Proven Steps to Eliminate Email Overload

» Wake Up Successful: How to Increase Your Energy and Achieve Any Goal with a Morning Routine

» 10,000 Steps Blueprint: The Daily Walking Habit for Healthy Weight Loss and Lifelong Fitness

» 70 Healthy Habits: How to Eat Better, Feel Great, Get More Energy and Live a Healthy Lifestyle

» Resolutions That Stick! How 12 Habits Can Transform Your New Year

Made in the USA
Middletown, DE
28 January 2018